'An engaging new book crammed full of easy to understand information for girls about ADHD and many related concerns. There are so many ideas and tips on how to manage the challenges of ADHD and survive the tricky teenage years. This book will be at the top of everyone's lists to recommend following an ADHD diagnosis in girls.'

– Dr Joanne Steer, clinical psychologist and co-author of
Helping Kids and Teens with ADHD in School

'"How do I start this essay?" "What should I do first?" "Why does everything feel so difficult?" if you are a teenager with ADHD these questions may be all too familiar. Offering information, guidance, tips and strategies on these and many other common struggles, this is a fun and lively book that takes the reader on an encouraging, upbeat and optimistic journey towards developing practical solutions to everyday frustrations. A fabulous read!'

– Valerie Ivens, ADHD coach, consultant and advocate

'This book is very informative, but still easy to read if you have ADHD. Skipped a chunk of text because your brain was being funky? Doesn't matter, the next section still makes sense and you can read what you missed later! Struggle with starting on large daunting blocks of text? Well, not to worry because all the essentials are in *bold* and you can go from there! And once you've finished reading this book, you'll have a better understanding of ADHD: its strengths, weaknesses and countermeasures. Clearly written, engaging and informative.'

– Anna Munt, history student at Cambridge,
owner of an ADHD brain

of related interest

Understanding ADHD in Girls and Women
Edited by Joanne Steer
Foreword by Andrea Bilbow OBE
ISBN 978 1 78775 400 3
eISBN 978 1 78775 401 0

The Spectrum Girl's Survival Guide
How to Grow Up Awesome and Autistic
Siena Castellon
Foreword by Temple Grandin
Illustrated by Rebecca Burgess
ISBN 978 1 78775 183 5
eISBN 978 1 78775 184 2

ADHD Is Our Superpower
The Amazing Talents and Skills of Children with ADHD
Soli Lazarus
Illustrated by Adriana Camargo
ISBN 978 1 78775 730 1
eISBN 978 1 78775 731 8

All Dogs Have ADHD
Kathy Hoopmann
ISBN 978 1 78775 660 1
eISBN 978 1 78775 66 18

THE TEENAGE GIRL'S GUIDE TO LIVING WELL WITH ADHD

Improve your Self-Esteem, Self-Care and Self Knowledge

Sonia Ali

Jessica Kingsley Publishers
London and Philadelphia

First published in Great Britain in 2022 by Jessica Kingsley Publishers
An Hachette Company

2

The illustrations in this book have been sourced from iStock.com from the
following users: Ilyabolotov, ngupakarti, Zdenek Sasek, RiMotions, bortonia,
Christian Horz, Pavel Sevryukov, msan10, Anna_Kolesnikova, hazimsn,
Mesut Ugurlu, Tetiana Garkusha, Olga Kurbatova, Tetiana Mykhailyk, Gwens
Graphic Studio, FrankRamspott, non-exclusive, Peacefully7, Yuliia_Hrozian,
Anna Semenchenko, asmakar, Sudowoodo, katflare, TonBoon, present, 9george,
Sonya_illustration, ericb007, Kongphop Petwichai, A-Digit, Aluna1, frimages,
S-S-S ,stcook, MarinaBH, eeewah, Serhii Brovko, Igor Levin, wehrmann69,
nadia_bormotova, ~Userba9fe9ab_931, mspoint, Amanda Goehlert.

A CIP catalogue record for this title is available from the
British Library and the Library of Congress

ISBN 978 1 78775 768 4
eISBN 978 1 78775 769 1

Printed and bound in Great Britain by TJ Books Limited

Jessica Kingsley Publishers' policy is to use papers that are natural,
renewable and recyclable products and made from wood grown in
sustainable forests. The logging and manufacturing processes are expected
to conform to the environmental regulations of the country of origin.

Jessica Kingsley Publishers
Carmelite House
50 Victoria Embankment
London EC4Y 0DZ

www.jkp.com

MIX
Paper from
responsible sources
FSC® C013056

Contents

Acknowledgements

Thank you to Jessica Kingsley Publishers and especially to Sean Townsend for his useful input on this project.

Thank you to all the women and girls with ADHD who have shared their experiences.

To Boyko, Olivia and Felix, thanks for your support. Thank you to Carmen and Ezzeddin.

Introduction

Awareness about **attention deficit hyperactivity disorder (ADHD)** has improved in recent years, but misconceptions about ADHD are still common.

It might surprise some people to learn that:

- **not everyone with ADHD is hyperactive or hyperactive in a noticeable way**

- **a person with ADHD is capable of high levels of concentration**

- **ADHD can affect girls as well as boys.**

Boys are four times more likely to be diagnosed with ADHD than girls before the age of 12, yet more adult women than men are diagnosed with ADHD.

What does this tell us?

It tells us that girls with ADHD often remain undiagnosed because **ADHD in girls is less well understood**.

Although ADHD impacts specific areas such as

- attention regulation

- hyperactivity and impulse control

- emotional regulation

- executive function skills.

not everyone is affected in these areas in the same way or presents in the same way.

People associate ADHD with young boys who are extremely hyperactive, but many people (girls and boys) do not fit this template.

Girls and boys are still **socialized differently** too (take a look at the messages on kids' T-shirts!) and this has a big impact on how you may choose to behave at times.

About you

- **You might have been told you were chatty or fidgety at school, so you worked hard to hide signs of your hyperactivity to avoid being told you were 'annoying' or 'too much'.**

- **Are you 'internally' hyperactive with a very busy mind** that is continually whirring with thoughts and songs that play on a loop?

- Perhaps you are not particularly hyperactive, but you do have challenges with regulating your attention.

- Maybe you have always been hyperactive and feel that hyperactivity in girls is not talked about enough.

- Perhaps you 'tune out' and daydream often and to others appear inactive rather than hyperactive?

- Maybe you are always striving to excel academically or 'people please' to overcompensate for what you feel are other challenges. (Evidence suggests that low self-esteem and anxiety is 2.5 times more common in girls with ADHD than boys with ADHD.)

The truth is that ADHD is more complex and varied than commonly understood!

This book aims to provide **information, support and useful tips** for any girl with ADHD (diagnosed or undiagnosed) so that they (you) can develop self knowledge and self-confidence. The book explores a range of issues, including some issues that might affect girls with ADHD disproportionately, such as low self-esteem and low self-image.

About me

I was a high school teacher for many years and later became a specialist advisory teacher for dyslexia and ADHD. Through my work, I learnt more about ADHD beyond the misconceptions – this helped me fully understand my own neuropsychology, which has been very empowering.

I hope this book will be help you feel **more empowered**.

How to read this book

- You can read this book from **cover to cover** or **pick and choose** chapters to read in any order.

- In each chapter, there are **questions for you to reflect on**, to think about and discuss – **you may choose to work through these questions with an adult mentor, parent, carer, or teacher**.

- Every chapter has a few **strategies and tips** to try out. Everyone with ADHD is individual, so the objective is to figure out what works best for you.

Read the chapter summaries below to find out which chapters are relevant.

CHAPTER 1: ATTENTION DEFICIT? HYPERACTIVITY DISORDER?

- How is **attention regulation** affected when you have ADHD?

- **Activity for reflection** – tick the statements you most agree with in a questionnaire to learn more about how your attention is affected.

- **At home** – core strategies to help you manage and complete homework and revision tasks.

- **In class** – explore some strategies to help you regulate attention during lessons and what your teachers can do to help.

- **Hidden hyperactivity** – what are the different ways you can be hyperactive?

- **Activity for reflection** – tick the statements that most apply to you to find out in what way you are hyperactive, if at all.

- **Strategies to help you channel hyperactivity in class** – learn about strategies such as movement breaks, doodling and fidget tools.

- **End-of-chapter thoughts** – recap on what you have learnt in this chapter and what your next steps will be.

CHAPTER 2: EXECUTIVE FUNCTIONING AND ADHD

- What is executive functioning? Find out about how executive functioning can be affected when you have ADHD.

- **Activity for reflection** – rank the statements to find out what areas of executive functioning are most difficult/ challenging to you.

- **Strategies to support executive functioning skills:**
  - o Tips for **working to deadlines** – such as 'task chunking' and 'task timing'.
  - o Tips for dealing with **object impermanence** – what to do when you often lose things or forget where you put them at school and at home.
  - o **Timekeeping** with ADHD – tips to help you process and judge the passing of time and what to do if you are always late for appointments and meeting friends.

- **Why you might act first and think later:**
  - o **Activity for reflection** – tick the statements you agree with to find out if you have traits of impulsivity.
  - o **What is working memory?** Learn about how working memory can affect how impulsively you take decisions.

- **End-of-chapter thoughts** – recap on what you have learnt in this chapter and what your next steps will be.

CHAPTER 3: THE STRENGTHS OF ADHD

- **The 'disco ball effect' and working to your strengths** – learn what helps your strengths shine through.

- **ADHD strengths:**
  - o **Creative thinking/divergent thinking** – what is the link between ADHD and creative thinking? Find out about what creative thinking and divergent thinking

are and how to explore your creative thinking strengths.

- o **Activity for reflection** – consider some questions to help you understand the ways in which you are a creative thinker.
- o **Quick thinking under pressure** – why might an individual with ADHD be good at thinking under pressure?
- o **Activity for reflection** – consider and discuss these questions to help you think about how you function under pressure.

- **Hyper-focus:**
  - o **What is hyper-focus** and how can you channel hyper-focus to avoid burnout?
  - o **Activity for reflection** – what motivates you to put a lot of effort into a task? Rank the statements in order.

- **Humour and a sense of fun:**
  - o **ADHD and humour** – why small talk just does not cut it!
  - o Top tips for **social fatigue and listening better** during a conversation.

- **Energy and enthusiasm:**
  - o Why your **energy and enthusiasm** can be invaluable.
  - o **Activity for reflection** – keep a positive journal.

- **End-of-chapter thoughts** – questions to help you reflect on what you have learnt and what strategies you will try.

CHAPTER 4: YOUR WANDERING MIND

- What are the **pros and downsides of mind wandering**?
  - Learn about the different types of **mind wandering**, so that you can be aware of what your mind is doing when it wanders. The traffic light system can help you.

- **Green light** – positive examples of mind wandering:
  - **Free, associative thinking** – learn how this type of thinking can help you.
  - **Creative thinking** – what is this type of thinking and how is it beneficial?
  - **Controlled and goal-oriented thinking**.

- **Amber light** – proceed with caution with this type of mind wandering:
  - **Daydreaming** – learn about why you might daydream and when and why daydreaming can become maladaptive (problematic).

- **Red light** – stop:
  - **Ruminating** – what is rumination and how can it affect your mental health?
  - **Worrying and catastrophizing** – what are the signs of excessive worry and catastrophizing?
  - Tips to manage **excessive worry and rumination**.

- **Obsessive compulsive disorder** (OCD) and ADHD:
  - **What is and isn't OCD** – follow the link to learn more about OCD.

- **End-of-chapter thoughts** – questions to help you reflect on what you have learnt and what strategies you will try.

CHAPTER 5: EMOTIONS AND HYPERSENSITIVITY

- **ADHD and intense emotions** – learn about how your emotions can be affected by ADHD.

- **Rejection sensitivity** – what is it and how might it affect you?

- **Approaches to help you manage rejection sensitivity**.

- **Anger:**
  - **Activity for reflection** – how do you manage feelings of anger?
  - **Controlled versus uncontrolled anger** –why controlled anger can be beneficial, but uncontrolled anger can be damaging.
  - Tips and ideas to help you **manage your anger**.
  - **Activity for reflection** – how to deal with strong emotions. Follow the video link to learn more strategies that you can use.

- **Love and romantic relationships:**
  - **Learn about limerance** and why you might obsess about a crush (celebrity or someone you know).
  - **Activity for reflection** – a quiz to find out how easily you become infatuated.
  - **Limerance** – what to think about.

- **More about ADHD and hypersensitivity:**
  - o Find out about links between **ADHD and hypersensitivity**.
  - o **Activity for reflection** – are you a hypersensitive person?
  - o Learn about **sensory processing and autism** – who to speak to and what to read if you think you are autistic.

- **End-of-chapter thoughts** – questions to help you reflect on what you have learnt and what strategies you will try.

CHAPTER 6: SELF-ESTEEM

- **Activity for reflection** – take the questionnaire to find out how self-critical you are.

- **Self-esteem and ADHD** – find out how self-esteem can be affected when you are a girl with ADHD.

- **Contingent self-esteem** – learn about what contingent self-esteem is and why you might experience it.

- **Activity for reflection** – take the questionnaire to find out if your self-esteem is contingent.

- **The pillars of good self-esteem** – what are the hallmarks of true self-esteem?

- **Seven ways to develop true self-esteem** – read the strategies and complete the activities.

- **End-of-chapter thoughts** – recap on what you have learnt in this chapter and what your next steps will be.

CHAPTER 7: SELF-CARE

- **What is self-care?** What does self-care mean?

- **Self-care non-negotiables** for anyone with ADHD – what are the four self-care non-negotiables? Take the questionnaire to help understand if you live with the self-care non-negotiables in place.

- **Learn healthy coping mechanisms** – learn about healthy coping mechanisms that help you become centred.

- **Sleep and ADHD** – find out how ADHD can affect sleep and what approaches you can take to help you improve your sleep.

- **Unhealthy coping mechanisms** – learn about unhealthy coping mechanisms, such as functioning anxiety and addictive pleasure-seeking activities.

- **Activity for reflection** – find out if your pleasure-seeking activity has become addictive.

- **Are you 'mental health aware'?**
  - **Anxiety** – follow the link to find out about anxiety.
  - **Tips and links to help you manage feelings of panic** and to 'ground yourself'.
  - **Trauma and ADHD** – what to do if you have experienced trauma and how to identify post-traumatic stress disorder.
  - **Depression** – follow the links to learn more about how to seek help for depression.

- **End-of-chapter thoughts** – reflect on what you have learnt and what you would like to do going forward.

CHAPTER 8: LIFE AFTER SCHOOL

- **Common stumbling blocks after school** – learn about sone obstacles you might encounter, such as overwhelm and adapting to new structures.

- **The value of the journey** – discover five top tips to help you navigate life after school, including dealing with money matters and eating healthily.

- **End-of-chapter thoughts** – recap on the ideas of the chapter.

6–12 MONTHS LATER: RE-EVALUATING YOUR SELF KNOWLEDGE

This short chapter will help you recap and reflect on what you now understand about yourself and identify what kind of external support and self-learning you are seeking to take steps forward.

one

ATTENTION DEFICIT? HYPERACTIVITY DISORDER?

The name **attention deficit hyperactivity disorder** is very misleading.

The word **deficit** suggests a **lack of something**. Not enough. Yet when you have ADHD, it can often feel like you have **too much attention** focused on **so many different things**!

Have you ever felt that your mind is full of hundreds of unrelated thoughts zooming around in your head like flies at a buffet?

FLY

Other times, you might be so focused on what you are doing (this could be gaming or a hobby or interest) that you find it very hard to stop and you remain intensely focused for hours.

And then there are those other times…when you cannot concentrate at all.

You try to do your homework or revision. You've got your books ready, you are sitting at your desk, **but your mind darts about like a butterfly**.

You daydream or scroll through your phone.

Or listen in to a neighbour talking loudly on the street outside.

Any distraction will grab your attention until evening falls and you have barely touched your homework.

Your attention is not in deficit.

Your attention is difficult to control and regulate.

Imagine what it would be like to have a wild animal for a pet and take it for a walk on a lead. Wild animals don't follow orders – they follow their instinct! Your attention is like a wild animal, following a trail, sniffing out excitement.

Why does your attention work in this way?

The answer is **brain chemistry**.

When you have ADHD, you generally have lower levels in your brain of two neurotransmitters called dopamine and norepinephrine (also known as noradrenaline in the UK). Neurotransmitters are chemicals that travel around all the regions of your brain passing messages to your nervous system.

These two neurotransmitters are really useful for igniting and maintaining attention:

- **Norepinephrine** helps 'fire up' and maintain your attention.

- **Dopamine** is the neurotransmitter that gives you a sense of reward and satisfaction from a task. That is why dopamine is often called the 'pleasure neurotransmitter'. Even the anticipation of pleasure can motivate you to do a task.

Because there is lower baseline level of these two neurotransmitters in your brain, **you will always be pulled** towards activities that are interesting and exciting to raise your level of dopamine and norepinephrine.

Activities that are urgent and need to be completed under pressure will become easier to do (which may explain why you leave tasks until the last minute!).

You could say that you have a low boredom threshold.

Stimulant medications used to treat ADHD increase the levels of one or both neurotransmitters. Visit www.nhs.uk/conditions/attention-deficit-hyperactivity-disorder-adhd/treatment to learn more.

There are upsides to how your brain works!

- **Your busy and curious brain is fantastic at thinking up new ideas, making you a very creative thinker.**
- **When you are really engaged in what you are doing, you are capable of incredible levels of concentration and enthusiasm.**

Read **Chapter 3: The Strengths of ADHD** and **Chapter 4: Your Wandering Mind** to learn more about the strengths of the way your ADHD brain works and how to maximize those strengths.

Activity for reflection

Let's think about how your attention regulation affects you.

Read the statements below. Which statements most apply to you? Which statement describes the area of most challenge for you?

1. **I put off tasks such as homework or school assignments until the very last moment and often don't get them finished on time.**

2. **I daydream a lot during the day at school, and then lose track of what is going on in lessons.**

3. **I find it really hard to get started on most school and homework, and I just avoid doing tasks completely.**

4. **I can get started with new projects, but I lose interest after a while.**

5. **When I am really interested in something, I find it hard to stop and can spend hours on it at any time, unless someone reminds me to stop.**

6. **I get so easily distracted by any noise or thoughts when I am trying to do something. I can only work in near silence.**

What did you learn?

If you chose 1, 2, 3, 4 and 6, read the strategies in this chapter.

Number 5 describes **hyper-focus**, which can be really useful, but you also need to take care not to burn out – read more about hyper-focus in **Chapter 3: The Strengths of ADHD**.

What strategies help with attention regulation?

HOMEWORK AND REVISION

Completing homework and revision, especially when it's on a subject that doesn't interest you, can be a real challenge.

The following strategies and approaches can help you.

1. Break a task into smaller parts

Sitting at your desk and realizing you have to complete 30 maths equations or a 1000-word essay can seem like a **massive** and **insurmountable** task.

You may be so daunted by how big the task is that you put off doing it for as long as possible. Instead, try this:

> **Break a big task into smaller tasks and set yourself one small task at a time.**

For example: 'I will write the first paragraph of the English essay' or 'I will answer four of the maths questions.'

This approach will make completing a task more achievable. You can do the next small task the following day or after a break.

2. Work in short blocks of time

This is a similar strategy to the one above, except now you are splitting up a task into smaller units of time.

> **Set your timer for a fixed period of time – it could be 10 minutes, 15 minutes or 25 minutes – and work for that duration. After the time is up, have a short break.**

You can begin again for the same amount of time until the task is finished or work on the task for short bursts of time every day.

3. Brain breaks are a must

Forcing yourself to be productive when every fibre of your mind and body is fighting it is counterproductive. If your concentration is fading, it is a sign that **your brain needs to recharge**.

Instead:

Leave your desk and do something different for 10, 15, or 20 minutes:

- **have a shower or bath**
- **bake**
- **chat to someone in your house**
- **watch a TV comedy show.**

After the time is up, attempt the task again.

Remember, if you are under a lot of stress or are feeling very tired, you may need a longer break. Read **Chapter 7: Self-Care** to learn about how to spot and manage exhaustion and chronic stress.

4. Study on the move

It is a common mistake to think that in order to study, you must be sitting at a desk.

Sitting at your desk may be slowing you down!

> **Moving about can help us think and concentrate better. You may be stuck for ideas and discover that if you go for a walk, the change of scene will help you think more clearly again.**

Before or during an intense period of study:

- Go for a walk. As you are walking, think about the task you need to do. If an idea comes to you, jot it down on your phone or record it.

- If you do need to do some written work at your desk, try to leave the room during your break.

5. Use assistive technology

You don't always have to use pen and paper or word-process your written work. You can speed up some tasks by using technology.

- **Download Google Docs on your phone if**

you have one, and write notes and ideas whenever they come to you (on the bus, on the train).

- **Use speech-to-text on your laptop to record ideas quickly.**

6. Find a study or revision buddy

Working with someone can help you stay focused. Even working alongside a parent/carer may be helpful and deter you from getting distracted.

7. Work in a library

Sometimes there are too many distractions and home comforts in your own house. The silence and lack of distractions in a library might help you keep on task. Can you work in a school library for 30 minutes some days?

8. Does music help?

Some tasks require lots of deep thought. Other tasks are quite mundane and may not require full concentration. **It may be easier for you to get those tasks done quickly by listening to music.**

LESSONS AND LECTURES

In school it can be a really hard to keep focused and avoid

'tuning out' or getting distracted during lessons. **School lessons can feel soooo long.**

Poor sleep the night before or any worries you have will also drain your energy, making it even harder to concentrate. It is really important to remember you can ask for adaptations and you can get support.

Some of the strategies suggested for self-study can also be used in lessons.

Speak to your SENCO (special educational needs coordinator) or any teacher and explain what helps you at home. For example, **you may feel that sometimes you need a brain break to allow you to pause and recharge during longer lessons**.

> **During a brain break, you may doodle for a while or simply look out of the window!**

Task adaptations

Some learning requires frequent practice to improve. These kind of tasks can be **really under-stimulating** if you have ADHD. A task that requires no creativity will be harder for you. **If your SENCO and teachers know that you have ADHD, it can be useful to begin having conversations about what kind of task is really hard for you to focus on and how some tasks can be adapted – for example, you might try creating a poster or mind map to show what you learnt in a lesson instead of writing a summary paragraph.**

Hidden hyperactivity

When many people think of ADHD, the first image that frequently still comes to mind is that of a small boy who cannot sit still and bounces around with never-ending energy. **But you can be hyperactive in different ways, some of which are less obvious, such as being very chatty or tapping your feet or twirling your hair or drumming your fingers** on the table.

There are three presentations of ADHD:

- inattentive

- hyperactive/impulsive

- combined.

Most girls are diagnosed with the **inattentive** presentation because they do not show obvious signs of hyperactivity, **but many girls may experience an internalized, mental hyperactivity – a mind that is so busy and noisy it can be hard to relax or fall asleep at night.**

 "Often I have a song playing in my head on a loop as well as several thoughts firing off at the same time."

 "I find it so hard to fall asleep at night because my mind is always whirring and busy. Sometimes, I daydream to fall asleep."

Activity for reflection

Do you think that you are **physically hyperactive** or do you feel that your hyperactivity is more **internalized**? Do you feel that you show signs of both physical and internalized hyperactivity or maybe you are **not hyperactive at all**?

Read through these statements below and decide which most apply to you?

1. **My mind is always busy: there is often a song playing in my head and lots of self-talk. I have trouble sleeping at night because I cannot get my brain to quieten down.**

2. I find it very hard to sit still and always feel like moving around or doing something active.

3. I need to do a lot of sport or walking – otherwise, I don't know what to do with my energy.

4. I often feel tired and like to rest.

5. I look around a lot and am very chatty in conversations.

6. Sometimes I don't want to talk much and prefer to be on my own and daydream.

If you chose 3, 4 and 6, you may experience **physical hyperactivity**.

If you chose 1, 2, and 5 but not 3 and 4, your hyperactivity is often **internalized**.

You may find that you may have a combination of all of the above.

STRATEGIES TO HELP YOU CHANNEL HYPERACTIVITY IN CLASS

When you lose focus in class, you will be more likely to fidget or chat. This is often the first sign that you're not stimulated enough and are losing concentration.

Try some of these strategies:

1. Movement breaks

Speak to your SENCO to agree some movement breaks during the day.

How this works will need to be agreed in advance. You might agree that you can use a movement break pass twice a day for ten minutes.

> **During a movement break, you might walk around the school grounds or carry out an errand for a teacher.**

2. Doodling and fidget tools

It is often incorrectly assumed that if you aren't looking at whoever is speaking, you aren't listening. In actual fact...

> **Some people find it easier to listen and filter out distractions if they are doing something with their hands, such as doodling or using a fidget tool.**

Agree with a teacher what you will do – you might be given a separate book for doodling, for example.

End-of-chapter thoughts

- What new strategies would you like to try to help you with homework and in school?

- What strategies have worked for you in the past?

- Have you learnt anything new about attention and hyperactivity?

two

EXECUTIVE
FUNCTIONING
AND ADHD

Every musician in the London Philharmonic Orchestra is extremely talented and has learnt and practised a musical instrument for many, many years. One evening the orchestra did not sound quite right. Each section of the orchestra seemed out of synch with the others. The strings were too quiet. The woodwind instruments were too loud. The percussion was out of tune.

The conductor ran on stage, picked up the baton and began to conduct. At once, the music flowed harmoniously.

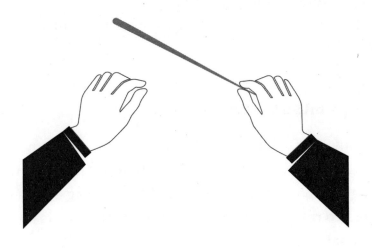

What is executive functioning?

Executive functioning is like a conductor or company director in your brain, overseeing and managing many different tasks in order to achieve a long-term aim.
Executive functioning skills include:

- organizing, planning and prioritizing a series of tasks

- managing your time and working towards deadlines

- sustaining your attention and commitment to a long-term goal

- managing your frustration levels with a task

- using working memory to consider several options before making a decision or acting on impulse.

Many of these tasks are initiated in a part of the brain called the **pre-frontal cortex**, which tends to show signs of less activity in people with ADHD as evidenced in **neuro-imaging (MRI) scans**.

IDEAS VERSUS REALITY

The irony of ADHD is that ADHD minds are constantly coming up with ideas. **Generating new ideas is an ADHD strength. Planning, organizing and completing all the tasks needed to realize your ideas, on the other hand, is much more challenging.**

"I wanted to plan my own 15th birthday party. I had really clear ideas about the music, the décor, the food, the cake..."

"But when I had to start ringing up people and sorting out dates and times and ordering things, it all got so complicated and overwhelming and I was going to give up. Fortunately, my mum stepped in."

THE GOOD NEWS

You can learn many strategies and approaches that will **support your executive functioning**.

As you get older and regularly use and adapt some of these approaches, completing certain tasks will become easier.

Activity for reflection

Read through these statements and put them in order of relevance to you. Which task is the most challenging?

- I miss deadlines at school or college more than my classmates do and I often need to ask for extensions to submit work.

- I am often late to meet people and I struggle to get to school/college on time in the morning.

- I don't like to organize meet-ups or events; I prefer others to do the organizing.

- I get worried about being late in the morning and this affects my sleep the night before.

- I have often forgotten to bring library books back or return forms before a due date.

- I often lose things or forget where I have left something.

- If I have a lot of work or deadlines to meet, I can get really overwhelmed with how much I need to do.

- I am very untidy, and my bag or room can be a mess unless I get help.

It is really useful to find support to help with executive function tasks. A mentor or teacher at your school can help you with the study skills approaches outlined in this chapter and gradually you will be able to use these strategies independently.

Strategies to support executive function skills

TIPS FOR WORKING TO DEADLINES

 "I always leave big deadlines until the last minute or I end up missing the deadline."

Most people with ADHD are familiar with **the last-minute rush. Leaving an essay or project until the last minute is one of the most common study/work patterns of people with ADHD.**

Sometimes, this works out fine, but often your output will be too rushed and not an accurate reflection of what you can really do. Other times, you will simply run out of time (highly likely!) and get in trouble for handing the work in late.

When you have a big task to do, and the deadline is still far off, it can be so tempting to put off doing any work until you are closer to the deadline.

Very often we **underestimate how long a task will take** and so the work is rushed or not completed in time.

Instead, with any big project or task, follow these **three steps:**

Step 1: Task chunking

Let's say the main task is: 'I need to write a 1500-word essay on a question about *Pride and Prejudice* for English.'

You need to chunk this big task into as many small tasks as you can think of – try to do this with a teacher or study buddy. For example:

1. I need to read the last 20 pages of *Pride and Prejudice*.

2. I need to read two essays to show evidence of wider reading.

3. I need to underline or highlight useful quotes in the essays and in the book.

4. I need to write a mind map or plan of each paragraph (I can work with someone to plan the essay).

5. I need to write the first 250 words or introductory paragraph.

6. I need to write paragraph 2.

Step 2: Task timing

On a separate day, look at the task chunking list you wrote. **Now, you will need to try to estimate how long it might take you to do each task.** Always **overestimate** the time it might take.

Task	Time needed
I need to read the last 20 pages of *Pride and Prejudice*.	1 hour
I need to read two essays to show evidence of wider reading.	1 hour
I need to underline or highlight useful quotes in the essays and in the book.	I hour
I need to write a mind map or plan of each paragraph.	45 minutes
I need to write the first 250 words or introductory paragraph.	40 minutes
I need to write paragraph 2.	40 minutes

Step 3: Task plotting

Buy or make a **calendar** of the month.

   Now, you will need to fill in your planner day by day, working back from the deadline. You can even plan days off if you have enough time until the deadline.

   Example:

February 2021

Monday	Tuesday	Wednesday	Thursday	Friday	Saturday	Sunday
1	2	3	4	5	6	7
8	9 Read the rest of the book (1 hour)	10 Read 1 essay for wider reading (30 minutes)	11 Read 1 essay for wider reading	12 Underline useful quotes	13 Break	14 Start the plan
15 Write the plan	16 Write introduction	17 Write paragraph 2	18 Write paragraph 3	19 Write paragraph 4	20 Write paragraph 5	21 Break
22 Write paragraph 6	23 Write paragraph 7	24 Write last paragraph (30 minutes)	25 **DEADLINE!**	26	27	28

What if I miss a day or I am not in the mood one day?

That is absolutely fine because you have allowed yourself down time to catch up and you only have to work for **small bursts** of time each day.

Enlist someone to help you map out your actions – working this way will take practice. **It may be useful to have a study coach or study buddy who can help you chunk big tasks into small tasks and keep to a schedule.**

If you have a diagnosis of ADHD in the UK, you can receive Disability Student Allowance after the age of 18, which allows you to access support from a study skills tutor. **A study skills support tutor can help you plan your time in areas related to study skills and time management.**

Tips for dealing with object impermanence

 "I am always losing, misplacing and forgetting where I have put things."

Do you find that you often **struggle to find things** and often have to replace books or stationery?

Do you forget to return library books all the time and end up having to pay a fee because you cannot find them?

Losing or forgetting items is a really common occurrence for people with ADHD. Sometimes it can end up being expensive as you have to pay late fees or pay to replace items you have lost.

AT SCHOOL

- Ask teachers to **print out homework tasks** which you place in an A4 wallet.

- **To avoid forgetting to bring the correct exercise books for each subject, colour-code your exercise books according to the day of the week** – for example, all the books you need to bring in on Monday will have a red sticker on the spine. OR **keep exercise books at school and do homework on paper and put into an A4 wallet.**

- **If you don't have a locker at school, ask the SENCO if you can store some belongings in a specific classroom or office, so that you do not have to constantly remember to bring them in.**

AT HOME

- **Label drawers** with clothes that you need to find easily – for example, underwear, socks.

- Ensure you **have a separate shelf or box for library books** only, so that they are not mixed with your own books.

- **Put items that you use and lose often into trays or open storage and label them.**

- Hang gym bags on a hook near the front door.

- **Keep a tray for homework tasks that you need to do and one tray for tasks that you have completed.** Put this tray somewhere very accessible, such as on your desk.

A place that 'looks' tidy with everything hidden away is often really unhelpful.

Instead, **think about storage that is very easy to get to such as open trays and boxes that you can dump items in easily as soon as you walk into the house**. Labelling these trays can be very useful, so that you can find thing easily.

Timekeeping with ADHD

 "I am always late or in a panic about being late!"

- Do you sometimes feel that you operate on a different timeframe to everybody else?

- **Does your mind wandering lead you to zone in and out of external reality and lose a continuous sense of the passing of time?**

- **You might feel that time is really slooooow when you are in a boring lesson, but time suddenly feels too fast when you have more than one appointment to keep in the day and you are needing to rush.**

Some of our attitudes to time can depend on cultural norms, too. Approaches to timekeeping are more rigid in some countries than others. However, **there are many situations in which being on time is really important**. If your exam is at 9.00 am and you arrive at 9.30, you won't get that time back to finish you answers.

TIPS FOR GETTING TO AN APPOINTMENT ON TIME

- **Prepare as much as you can the day before an important appointment:**
  - o choose what clothes you will wear

- o pack your bag
- o check the bus timetable
- o set more than one alarm clock, if necessary.

- **Have clocks everywhere.**
  - o Your concept of time is not intrinsic. **You need to see or hear the passing of time.** Have a clock in every room, if possible.

- **Overestimate the time needed to complete a journey.**
  - o Add extra time onto a journey time.

TIPS FOR MEETING FRIENDS

How many times have you kept a friend waiting because you were late? Or arrived late to a party or gathering after everyone else?

If you accept that, even with the best intentions, you may still be late, there are steps you can take to avoid putting people out too much.

- **Think about safety and comfort. Always arrange to meet somewhere safe and interesting for whoever needs to wait.** You could arrange to meet in a shopping mall or offer to pick them up from their house.

- **Be honest. If you know the person well, you can be upfront and tell them that you find it challenging to manage time.** Friends can also help – a good friend will make suggestions about where you can meet that will be easier for you both. **Show appreciation for their patience.**

- **Don't beat yourself up.** There are other ways in which you are and can be a good friend.

It may be comforting to know that your sense of time does get better. A person in their 40s with ADHD will have a better grasp of time than they did when they were in their teens!

Why you might act first and think later

Activity for reflection

Read through and tick any statements that are relevant to you:

- **I am a 'thrill seeker' and will often take risks for the buzz.**

- **I have often overreacted to a post on social media or a comment someone made and then regretted it later.**

- **I often act before I think, which gets me into trouble.**

- **I blurt out things in conversations or in class, without pausing first, and it can get quite awkward.**

- **If I want to do something, I will usually do it without thinking about the consequences.**

Did you say YES to more than four statements?

When you experience impulsive traits with ADHD, you will find it hard to pause and think before acting on a strong impulse or emotion. This can lead to moments of fun and spontaneity or acts of kindness and quick thinking. You may reach out to someone who seems sad when everyone else is too shy to do the same, or you may react very quickly to a potential threat that requires an immediate response.

Impulsivity can also present you with many challenges. You can end up taking actions on the spur of the moment that you later regret or take risks that can be dangerous.

WHAT IS THE LINK BETWEEN IMPULSIVITY AND ADHD?

A really important brain function for impulse control is called **working memory**. Working memory is the executive functioning skill that allows you to hold thoughts in your mind and ponder an idea before you act on it.

Some people with ADHD will have a smaller working memory capacity and show less activity in parts of the brain that inhibit strong impulses.

WHAT IS WORKING MEMORY?

Imagine you are walking from school or college and you spot a handful of £20 notes in the middle of a very busy road.

Your immediate impulse is to dash across the street and grab the money – after all, you are flat broke. At this moment, you are in danger. **Cars are passing very fast, and if you act on this impulse, you are taking a big risk.**

In moments like this, the fleeting thoughts that cross your mind can help you pause before you run on to the road. Thoughts such as:

- What if I trip up and cannot get out of the way of the passing cars?

- I nearly got run over the last time I rushed for the bus. What if I get run over this time?

- If I miscalculate the speed of that car, it will hit me!

The larger your working memory capacity, the more thoughts you can have before acting on impulse, which will influence your decision.

IMPULSIVITY AND SELF-CARE

Self-care is vital to helping you **manage impulsivity**.

> **You are more likely to act on impulse when you are bored or over-tired or in low mood.**

Read **Chapter 5: Emotions and Hypersensitivity** and **Chapter 7: Self-Care** to learn more about your emotions and how to look after your emotional and mental health.

End-of-chapter thoughts

- Did you learn anything new about executive functioning skills? If so, what?

- Are there any areas of executive functioning that you would like more support with? What areas are these?

- Do you think that the way your room is organized at home could be changed to make it easier for you to find things?

three

THE STRENGTHS
OF ADHD

Have you ever seen a disco ball in broad daylight?

It looks quite dull and obsolete, hanging from the ceiling.

When night falls and you turn the spotlights on, a disco ball undergoes a startling transformation – hundreds of tiny specks of coloured light dance on the walls, the ceiling and the floor reflected off its mirrored surface.

A disco ball transforms a room.

The disco ball effect

When you have ADHD, your strengths can shine very brightly.

Can you think of a time when your strengths revealed themselves clearly to you and perhaps to others around you? Perhaps your energy and enthusiasm got a project off the ground or your creative ideas were taken up during a group brainstorm session in a lesson?

Working to your strengths

Award winning journalist, Lisa Ling, who has ADHD, said in an interview:

 "I have always had a bit of a difficult time focusing on things that aren't interesting to me. When I'm immersed in a story, then I feel like I can laser focus."

Lisa Ling found that journalism was inherently interesting to her and allowed her to work to her strengths.

The rapper and music producer, will.i.am, who has ADHD said:

 "One thing I have learnt about ADHD is that you are always moving and thinking about a whole bunch of things. But those traits work well for me in studios and in meetings about creative ideas."

> **If you are in the right environment and engaged in activities that interest you, many ADHD traits become valuable strengths.**

ADHD strengths

You will have **individual traits and qualities** that are specific to you. **Everyone with ADHD is as individual as anyone without ADHD.**

It is also the case that some traits associated with ADHD can be advantageous. **Differences in the brain structure and brain chemistry associated with ADHD are linked to the following strengths.**

CREATIVE THINKING/DIVERGENT THINKING

The news is out! **There is clear, scientific research-based evidence to prove that people with ADHD find most types of creative thinking easier than people without ADHD!**

Now, this is not to say that everyone with ADHD is infinitely more 'creative' than everyone else – not every artist, writer or inventor has ADHD! **Instead, your mind is inclined to generate innovative, original and inventive ideas more readily.**

Creative thinking includes:

- **divergent thinking** – the ability to formulate ideas that are original and break with convention

- **the ability to overcome knowledge barriers** – to find solutions and 'join the dots' without the need for plenty of prior knowledge

- **associative thinking** – making connections between different concepts in order to formulate an original idea.

Creative thinking skills are a real advantage

Creative thinking is really useful in many areas of life and work and does not just apply to the creative arts (drawing, painting, fiction writing, etc.). For example, creative thinking could be useful for **problem solving**. Ever seen those interesting space-saving items of furniture? That's an example of creative thinking in product design.

> **When you have ADHD, it's important that you find different ways to channel your creative thinking skills. Many ADHDers find that having a creative outlet is really important for their mental health.**

Activity for reflection

- Can you think of a time when you used creative thinking to find a solution?

- What creative hobbies or activities do you currently participate in?

- Would you like to try more creative activities? If so, what would you like to try? If not, think about the kind of creative activities that might interest you? In **Chapter 6: Self-Esteem**, you can answer a questionnaire to find out about the sort of creative activities you might enjoy.

QUICK THINKING UNDER PRESSURE

Do you find that you often leave a homework task or an assignment until the very last minute? When you are under pressure, does your focus becomes razor sharp?

If you answered YES to these questions, you certainly won't be the only person with ADHD who does.

People with ADHD often find it easier to concentrate and perform well on a task when they feel **a sense of urgency or pressure**. You may choose to live on the edge a little and often meet deadlines at the last minute – which may or may not always work out!

This ability to function well under pressure can be an advantage.

In an emergency, you might be the one who can think quickly and make decisions, while those around you panic.

The urgency of an extreme situation clears away any fog of indecision, making it easier to act quickly in an emergency.

Activity for reflection

- Do you find it easier to make decisions 'on the hoof' rather than making long-term plans?

- Think about a time when the decisive action you took was vital in a situation. Perhaps, you acted in response to something you felt was wrong or unjust? What actions did you take in that situation?

HYPER-FOCUS

When you have ADHD, there will be days when you find it extremely hard to begin any task and your attention buzzes around like a bumble bee. **There will be other days when your focus and concentration can best be described as turbo-powered.**

You may have the capacity to become extremely focused on an activity that interests you to the point that you find it hard to stop. This is often referred to as hyper-focus. When you are really engaged in what you are doing, you can experience waves of intense productivity.

 "When I am drawing a new portrait, I can work for hours and hours without stopping."

How to channel your hyper-focus and avoid burnout

When you have ADHD, your pattern of working is not linear and uniform. Instead, **you may experience waves of heightened productivity followed by periods of inactivity.**

When you are hyper-focused, you can achieve a lot in a
short space of time, but working this way can also leave
you feeling exhausted and you may even neglect to drink
or eat. Be mindful to follow some simple routines of self-care
during periods of intense hyper-focus:

- Set an alarm to remind you to stop and drink fluids and
  eat (see **Chapter 8: Life After School** for suggestions for
  easy-to-make foods).

- After an intense session or period of hyper-focus, allow
  yourself rest time for a day or for a few days.

**WARNING: You can also hyper-focus on pleasure-seeking
activities that can be addictive such as excessive social
media use or gambling.** You can read more about self-care
and unhealthy coping mechanisms in **Chapter 7: Self-Care.**

Activity for reflection

Think of the last activity you did when you were **hyper-focused**. What was the motivation for you to keep working? What was the driving force to keep you engaged for so long?

Think about what motivates you to put a lot of effort into a task? Rank these in order:

- **I like to challenge and push myself.**

- **I am motivated the most by the idea of helping others or improving the state of the environment.**

- **I feel motivated by creating something new.**

- **I am motivated by learning new things about what interests me.**

- **I am motivated by being the best I can be.**

- **Encouragement from others is really useful for me and helps motivate me.**

When you are motivated to do something, you will be more likely to work very hard at it, but be careful that your motivation is not driven by a need to meet the approval of others. Read **Chapter 6: Self-Esteem** to learn more about this.

HUMOUR AND A SENSE OF FUN

You probably find small talk really dull. Instead, **you prefer conversations that are profound and absorbing. Some conversations will have you zoning out unless you are able to inject some humour and passion into the interaction.** Many ADHDers have a playful sense of fun and can be humorous or interesting conversationalists for this reason.

If you are usually chatty and animated in conversation, there may be other times when you feel depleted of energy and are not in the mood to socialize. **It is fine to follow the ebb and flow of your mood.**

Top tip for social fatigue

If you have arranged to meet a friend but feel tired and frazzled, you can arrange a low-key catch up, such as watching a film. It is fine to say that you need time to decompress. **Don't feel you have to perform a version of yourself when you don't feel it. This will tire you out.**

Top tip for listening

When you feel a high level of energy, you may worry that during conversations you talk over other people or interrupt them in your enthusiasm to speak. Try using some of these techniques to maintain balance in the conversation:

- **Ask questions after you have spoken** – 'Jo, I have been talking a lot. What do you think about…?', 'Jo, have you ever been to…?'

- **Fidget** – playing with a button or twirling a ring around your finger will help you wait until the other person has finished telling their story.

ENERGY AND ENTHUSIASM

Your thirst for new life experiences is infectious – others will be energized in the company of someone who is raring to get started on a project, for example. Creative thinking and enthusiasm combined can be a potent combination.

Activity for reflection

Keep a positive journal. It can be really tempting to focus on what we find hard rather than what is easy. Some ADHD traits are a two-sided coin – these traits can be a challenge and a strength, depending on the situation.

- Keep a journal to **recall situations when you recognized your strengths**. Example: 'Today in English, I created the role-play idea for our group and it went really well.'

- Record or write these experiences on a **weekly basis** or more often.

End-of-chapter thoughts

- Has learning more about some of the associated strengths of ADHD made you feel differently about having ADHD? How?

- Which strengths explored in this chapter do you identify most in yourself?

- What actions might you take in the future to explore or expand on your ADHD strengths? (Perhaps you will try to be less worried about being yourself in social situations, for example.)

four

YOUR WANDERING MIND

Everyone's mind wanders sometimes – who isn't thinking about something else when they're waiting for the bus or walking home?

When the external world becomes too dull, our brains will step up to entertain us. We will channel our attention away from the outside world and turn it inwards towards an internal landscape created by our thoughts. This is called mind wandering.

When you have ADHD, you will probably find your mind wandering far more frequently during the day than someone without ADHD.

 "There is always lots going on in my head – daydreams, thoughts, ideas, plans, songs playing on a loop – it keeps me entertained and tires me out too!"

The many pros of mind wandering

Mind wandering is a necessary part of being human. Humans are the only species whose mind wanders. Mind wandering allows us to **visualize and consider future scenarios** and to **innovate and create new ideas** from what has happened before.

People whose mind wanders more often tend to be creative thinkers; mind wandering allows them to flesh out new ideas and concepts before putting these ideas into action.

THE DOWNSIDE TO MIND WANDERING

A mind that wanders more easily can be prone to rumination, overthinking and worry. This type of thinking can increase the chances of experiencing anxiety or low mood. Sometimes, girls are diagnosed for ADHD only after visiting the doctor for help with anxiety or depression. Many girls with ADHD have experienced anxiety at some time.

TYPES OF MIND WANDERING

Mind wandering will take you to many wonderful places, but there can be risks, too.

One way of maintaining some control over your mind wandering is to become aware of what kind of mind wandering your brain is engaged in, so you can recognize if it is safe to continue or if you should try to stop your train of thought. Read about the **different types of mind wandering** below. They are grouped according to **this traffic light system** to help you understand what type of thinking is beneficial and which is harmful.

GREEN = safe to go

AMBER = pause and proceed if safe to do so

RED = STOP!

GREEN = safe to go

FREE, ASSOCIATIVE THINKING

While shampooing your hair, you imagine how much easier life would be with a shaved head, how cool you would feel in the summer and how much extra time you would have to do other things.

Your mind begins to reflect on all the many arbitrary concepts of beauty that exist, such as shaving hair on your legs yet growing hair on your head. You realize that trying to meet current beauty standards usually involves restricting your time or freedom. You continue to follow this train of thought until you experience a moment of **intense clarity** about beauty ideals – while you are in the shower…washing your hair.

Free thinking usually occurs when you are calm and under little external pressure. Your mind is free to roam and ponder any thoughts or ideas that pop up as there is very little conscious control. It's a bit like taking a hike in an area of natural beauty without a map.

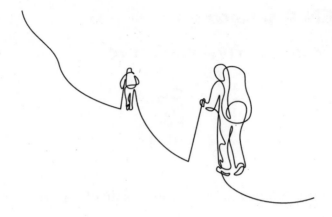

Free, associative thinking will lead you to make connections between disparate concepts and ideas, and it can be the **first step towards creative thought** and the inception of an original idea.

> **TOP TIP**
>
> If you are not experiencing much stress, allow yourself free-thinking time during the week. Your brain will appreciate this unstructured 'play time' and it could lead to creative inspiration.

CREATIVE THINKING

Creative thinking describes that lightbulb moment when a new idea pops into your head, usually after some time of free thinking or controlled thinking. Many people with ADHD are very familiar with the lightbulb moment and it can be an exciting and exhilarating experience to be struck by a novel idea.

Some of your ideas will ignite and fade away quickly – like a tiny shooting star.

Other ideas will have a longer shelf life and you will come back to work on them again and again.

Do you often doodle or write your own stories or ideas down?

Do you like creating art or recording sketches on video? Do you make things?

TOP TIP

Record your ideas.

Try to keep some of what you write or doodle in notebooks or record your ideas on video. An idea that occurred to you several years ago could be the seed of a future project.

CONTROLLED AND GOAL-ORIENTED THINKING

This is the most controlled type of mind wandering when you

are **actively planning next steps** on a current or potential project or task. You may visualize a desired outcome for a plan you have and will think about how to actualize this plan so that it become an action.

AMBER = pause and proceed if safe to do so

DAYDREAMING

> **Living in LA had changed Melissa. She looked different, she felt different. It had been four months since she had been back home and as the train stopped at the platform, her heart began to thump. What if they had not forgiven her? What if he'd moved on? (Becky Freeman, June 2019)**

This is not the opening paragraph of a novel by Becky Freeman or a scene from a film. If you Google 'story about Melissa by Becky Freeman', you will not come up with any results.

This is a scene from the plot of a week-long daydream that Becky Freeman has been completely invested in. This daydream includes a dramatic love story and moments of such heightened excitement and sadness that Becky has sometimes cried real tears.

Can daydreaming be good for you?

Daydreaming is linked to strong creative thinking skills – a daydreamer needs an active imagination to develop the technicolour stories that play out in their head. Some types of daydreaming may help people prepare for future situations by helping them visualize and enact possible outcomes. Other daydreams are pure indulgent fantasy that entertain.

 "I daydream quite a lot when I am doing anything that's a bit dull. It also helps me do tasks that don't require a lot of mental focus like washing dishes."

But what if your daydreaming becomes more and more frequent? What if it becomes hard to control how often and when you daydream?

Maladaptive daydreaming

Many girls with ADHD daydream a lot. These daydreams could be action-packed adventures that follow complicated plotlines over days or weeks. (Some people may return to familiar stories again and again over many years.)

When your daydreams are particularly absorbing, you

may end up hyper-focusing on the daydream and become addicted to this emotionally charged alternative world you have created. Hyper-focusing on a daydream requires you to completely tune out of your external reality for a long time and this can leave you feeling disconnected when your mind returns to the external reality again.

When daydreaming is really intense, it can be very **hard to switch it off**. You may spend a lot of time on your own, so that you can daydream, but afterwards you may feel strange and anxious.

The term maladaptive daydreaming describes daydreaming that becomes excessive and compulsive to the point that it affects your life negatively.

Signs of maladaptive daydreaming include:

- daydreaming for several hours during the day, often during the week

- difficulty controlling the urge to daydream at various points of the day

- replacing or preferring daydreaming interactions to real-life interactions.

If you have ADHD, especially the inattentive presentation, you may recall times when your daydreaming could be described as maladaptive.

Activity for reflection

- Do you think that you daydream too much some days?

- When are you more likely to daydream the most? (When you are bored? Tired? Stressed? Sad?)

- Do you use daydreaming as a comfort and a way of disassociating from real-life problems?

Why you may daydream too much at times

Excessive daydreaming can be a buffer against feelings of anxiety or worry or low self-esteem. A daydream could be providing temporary mental relief from how you feel in real life, but whatever is causing you to feel anxious, hurt, worried, low or unmotivated will not vanish if you daydream. You need to take concrete actions and find other coping mechanisms that allow you to process your feelings about your reality in a healthy way.

TOP TIP
If you notice that your daydreaming has recently become excessive and harder to control, read Chapter 7: Self-Care.

RED = STOP!

RUMINATING AND WORRYING

When you have ADHD, you have an enormous capacity **for creativity, fun and innovation**. But ADHD can also predispose you to **overthink, ruminate or experience an intense emotional reaction to rejection** or perceived rejection.

Girls with ADHD in particular, may internalize negative messages from society and ruminate about how they 'measure up' to external expectations. This pattern of thinking can have a hugely negative impact on self-esteem.

Do you often worry about how you look or your body shape? **Do you think about how others see you rather than how you feel about yourself?**

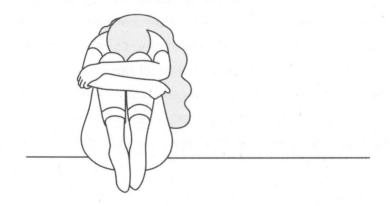

If you are over-tired, stressed or experiencing challenges in your personal life, you may 'tune out' of your external reality more often. The danger is that your mind wondering

will lead you down a few rabbit holes that can make you feel much worse.

Some types of mind wandering increase your stress and anxiety by creating a reality that is distorted and harmful to your sense of self and your outlook on life.

There are two types of thinking that girls with ADHD may be prone to:

Ruminating

Rumination means to 'overthink' and dwell on a situation that you have experienced. There is no real purpose to this type of thinking – you are not trying to find a solution. Instead, you may dwell on a comment you received until you become stuck in a loop. **For example, you may start to pick apart a comment on your Twitter page and begin to dwell on that comment. This will escalate into worrying about who would have seen it and what they would think about you.** This chain of thought can develop inexorably until you become convinced that you are hated or disliked by most people. Your perception of your external reality becomes **distorted and exaggerated. This altered perception is referred to as cognitive distortion.**

Worrying and catastrophizing

Worrying often follows a similar repetitive pattern to rumination except you become focused on an imagined future event that has **not happened or is not likely to**

happen – at least not how you imagine it to. **When you catastrophize, you imagine worst possible outcomes:**

 "What if Jane realizes she does not like me any more and I lose my best friend?"

"What if our plane crashes and we all die?"

It's easy to see how this thought process would drastically increase your anxiety levels.

Tips to manage excessive worry and rumination

No one has a stop or pause button in their brain that will instantly shut down a cycle of negative thinking. Instead, **you will have to very gradually take steps to re-connect with your external world and to do the activities that help you find enjoyment in the external world.**

1. **Recognize what life situations or experiences seem to trigger negative thinking** and build a repertoire of **self-care** during stressful periods in your life. Very often, what you are overthinking or worrying about is not the root cause of your feelings of stress. There may be deeper fears that you need to explore.

2. **Take practical action. Is there a concrete action you can take that will help alleviate or minimize some of your worry?** You might not always be able to take concrete steps to make a situation better, but even a small action can help you feel less helpless. In this case, always speak

to someone who can help you formulate practical steps to take and don't be afraid to ask for help and advice.

3. **Consider a 'talking therapy' to help you manage anxiety and low mood.** Sometimes traumatic events from your past may make it harder to process and deal with situations as they arise in your life. A past trauma may cause you to experience high levels of anxiety when something triggers a memory. Read **Chapter 7: Self-Care** for more information about where you can seek help for past trauma.

4. **Build your self-esteem. Low self-esteem may also make you prone to types of thinking that are overly self-critical.** You will read more about how to build your self-esteem in **Chapter 6: Self-Esteem.**

5. **Always seek support if you have felt unhappy or anxious for more than a few weeks.** In these situations, you can really benefit from receiving some **'talking therapy'** such as counselling or psychotherapy.

The following NHS website explains what **different types of talking therapy or counselling** are available. You should ask to see a regular doctor or speak to a designated professional at school so that you can begin a referral process for therapy:

www.nhs.uk/mental-health/talking-therapies-medicine-treatments/talking-therapies-and-counselling/types-of-talking-therapies

Obsessive compulsive disorder (OCD) and ADHD

There is a common misconception that **obsessive compulsive disorder (OCD)** is another type of mind wandering similar to rumination. It is not. While everyone may experience intrusive thoughts from time to time, OCD is a specific neurological condition and should be treated as such.

Signs of OCD include:

- frequent intrusive thoughts

- needing to follow certain precise rituals or a sequence of actions before beginning a number of activities.

Follow this link to find out more about OCD:

www.gosh.nhs.uk/conditions-and-treatments/conditions-we-treat/obsessive-compulsive-disorder

End-of-chapter thoughts

- What do you think you have learnt about mind wandering that you did not know before?

- Why do you think it is useful to develop an awareness of what your mind does when it wanders?

- What types of mind wandering have you engaged in the

most during the last few weeks? What do you think this tells you about how you are feeling?

- What three things would you try to do if you catch yourself ruminating or worrying too excessively?

five

EMOTIONS AND HYPERSENSITIVITY

Dear Diary,

Today, was hell on earth. I don't think I can go to school tomorrow – I just cannot deal with the hurt anymore.

Me, Elise and Jo were practising the song we are going to sing at the summer concert. Just as I start to sing my solo, who should walk past but Jake and Tyrese! Jake covered his ears and said really loudly, so that everyone could hear, 'Someone make her stop! My ears are bleeding. She's sooo bad!' He then began to imitate my singing. Elise and Jo were trying not to laugh. **I felt like I'd been punched in the stomach. I ran to the toilets after break and cried so hard. Elise and Jo told me no one meant any harm, but I don't think I will ever sing in front of anyone again!**

Hannah (Year 7) (US Grade 6)

Hannah eventually put this incident behind her, but she also cried in the morning before going to school and spent the day feeling like her world was crashing down around her.

It took her a few months to feel less self-conscious about singing in front of others.

ADHD and intense emotions

Do you feel that you experience emotions very intensely?
When you are happy, are you **really happy**, and when you are sad or angry, do you feel **extremely sad** or **extremely angry**?

When you have ADHD, you may feel that your emotions are always 'close to the surface'? Maybe you feel that you are very sensitive and feel things deeply? This emotional reactivity can be great if you experience something positive and the world feels beautiful – you probably have a huge capacity to enjoy life at these times. But what about those times when you are the butt of a joke or you receive criticism or someone hurts you? In these situations, you may feel a very deep sense of pain or hurt that can really floor you.

Rejection sensitivity

It is fairly common for people with ADHD to be **extremely sensitive to criticism** or even perceived criticism from others.

If you experienced criticism or you perceived rejection from others when you were younger, you may become hyper-vigilant to any signs of it again. This can change how you behave with others. You may become very cautious around others and come across as distant or experience social anxiety, often feeling as if you are being scrutinized and assessed by others often.

Let's be clear: **nobody** on the planet likes feeling rejected or criticized, but when you experience **rejection sensitivity**, the emotions you feel can be very intense. You might:

- **feel extremely sad and distraught** after receiving even a small negative comment or criticism, which subsides after a few hours or days.

- **believe that someone does not like you** or is being critical, even when there is no real evidence for this belief

- **ruminate over a comment you have received over and over and over** in your head until you feel very much worse about what they said

- **get really angry and lash out** at people if you are upset

- be told that you are **'too sensitive'**

- be extremely cautious and **on your guard** around people.

Rejection sensitivity is not exclusive to people with ADHD, but it is common in people with ADHD.

There is no magic quick-fix formula for managing rejection sensitivity. Instead, by taking the steps below, over time you will be better able to manage your feelings of rejection sensitivity.

APPROACHES TO HELP YOU MANAGE REJECTION SENSITIVITY

1. **Develop your self-esteem.** Low self-esteem may intensify your rejection sensitivity and make you more prone to **perceiving** a comment as rejection or criticism when it was not intended that way. Read **Chapter 6: Self-Esteem** to learn how to begin to build your self-esteem.

2. **Self-care.** Read **Chapter 7: Self-Care** to learn what daily and weekly practices can help you manage your emotional health.

3. **Talking therapy.** Rejection sensitivity will be more severe if you have experienced insecure attachment relationships with caregivers or you have been hurt in the past. Finding a therapist or counsellor to talk about your past experiences can help you better understand and manage

your feelings of rejection sensitivity. If you think that you may benefit from talking about past traumas, speak to your SENCO or a trusted adult about the steps to take to arrange this.

4. **Medication.** If you feel that you experience rejection sensitivity very often and severely, discuss this with your doctor or nurse prescriber.

Anger

It is healthy to feel angry if someone has hurt you. It is healthy to feel angry about injustice or mistreatment by others. Anger fuels social justice movements.

Anger can **mobilize** people to challenge inequality in society and to confront injustice.

In our relationships and friendships with others, extreme anger can be problematic. We may say nasty things and become cruel to someone when we are angry. We may lash out and sometimes even become physically aggressive.

If you do become very angry with another person, it may be hard for them to trust you.

Activity for reflection

Complete these sentences with an answer that is true to you:

- **When I am really angry, I tend to...**

- **I feel the most angry when...**

- **This makes me so angry because I feel...**

It can be very useful to think about what feelings drive our anger. Look at your answers above. What **feeling** or **type of actions from others** makes you feel the angriest?

CONTROLLED VERSUS UNCONTROLLED ANGER

Expressing controlled anger can be a useful form of communication in a relationship or friendship. Anger will help others understand why we are upset and what our boundaries are. **It is very important that we recognize the difference between controlled anger and uncontrolled anger,** so that we can learn what is an acceptable expression of anger and what is not.

Controlled anger

- You are able to communicate why you are upset and why you feel the way you do.

- You are able to hear and listen to the other person's point of view.

- You feel in control of your emotions.

Uncontrolled anger

- You have a strong impulse to hurt the other person emotionally or physically or to damage something.

- You are not able to communicate why you are angry.

- You are not in control of your anger.

Emotional regulation describes your ability to regulate strong emotions so that your thoughts are not flooded by emotion. Emotional regulation can be **harder when you have ADHD**, which means it can be harder for you to reflect before reacting.

 "Sometimes my emotional reactions get in the way of friendships. My friend cancelled a cinema trip recently because she had double-booked. I was so angry and hurt that I told her I did not want to be friends with her and that she was not a true friend, then I hung up on her when she tried to apologize. A few days later, I realized that I had overreacted. I remembered how nice she can be and I also remembered that I had once double-booked or cancelled some of our meetings and she had not made me feel too bad about it."

> **Showing controlled anger can be positive, but uncontrolled anger is never positive. There are many things that you can do to manage anger better.**

TIPS AND IDEAS TO HELP YOU MANAGE YOUR ANGER

1. Explore what triggers your anger

At the root of all anger is fear – **fear of being hurt**. This fear may be triggered in situations that remind us of past experiences. When you are calm, it may be useful to try to think about what makes you feel the most angry and why.

- What situations trigger the strongest feeling of anger in you?

- Can you think of past experiences that may have brought about these responses?

Think about these questions for a while. They can hold a key to helping you understand why you react the way you do in some situations and not others,

You may not always show outward signs of aggression when you are very angry. Instead, your strongest emotions might be 'swallowed up' and processed in ways that are self-destructive and result in feelings of low mood and despondency.

Talking therapies may help you untangle feelings that remain from you past. It can help you identify unprocessed feelings of anger from past trauma.

2. Recognize the physical signs of your anger when it is uncontrolled

When we are angry, a physiological reaction occurs in our body which causes our heart to beat faster, the palms of our hands to sweat and our muscles to tense up.

What does uncontrolled anger feel like to you? What physical sensations do you feel? If you learn to recognize these signs, you will be better able to take the next two actions.

3. Leave the scene

When your anger feels uncontrolled, it will be hard for you to think clearly. In this state, you are at great risk of doing or saying something that you will definitely regret later. The safest action you can take is to **go somewhere else** that is away from whoever or whatever is making you angry and wait until your anger feels controlled enough for you to communicate better. This is easier said than done and will take practice.

4. Go for a walk, run or do a go-to activity that helps calm you down

Physical activity such as walking or running could help expend some of that additional energy you will be feeling because of the increased levels of adrenaline in your body.

You may prefer to do something that helps distract you and calm you down, such as listening to music or playing a video game. **Find whatever it is that helps you feel calmer and make that a go-to activity.**

Activity for reflection

If you would like to learn more about how to deal with strong emotions, watch this video by ADHD YouTuber Jessica McCabe about rejection sensitivity and managing strong emotions:

www.youtube.com/watch?v=jM3azhiOy5E

After watching this video, try to answer the questions:

- What are the **4 Rs** that are recommended to help you manage very strong emotions?

- What **strategies** are suggested to help you manage strong feelings?

What do you think you will try to do when you feel strong anger?

Love and romantic relationships

When you have ADHD, you can easily hyper-focus on an area of interest. Sometimes, this 'interest' can be a person!
Evidence suggests that teens with ADHD are drawn to **'sensation-seeking' experiences**, such as developing infatuations about somebody. **This intense and all-encompassing feeling of infatuation for another person is sometimes called limerence.**

Activity for reflection

- Do you experience very intense infatuations towards others? (This may be people you know or a celebrity crush.)

- Do you find that you can hyper-focus on thinking about someone you like quite obsessively?

- Do you often feel drawn to relationships that are dramatic?

Limerence can be unrequited, in which case you may daydream a lot about the person who you have a crush

on and think about them obsessively. **Limerence may also be reciprocated and lead to a relationship.** It is important to recognize that the intense feelings you experience at the start of a relationship will eventually fade and evolve into something else. In that way, **infatuation is differentiated from the idea of genuine love because it is a finite experience**.

LIMERANCE – WHAT TO THINK ABOUT

In the early stages of a relationship, **be careful about making big decisions too quickly, especially if you are prone to acting on impulse**. You might consider dropping out of a college course to join your new partner in another city. Before making a decision, ask yourself some questions:

- When these intense and exciting feelings subside, will I be as happy with this person?

- Am I drawn to the intense feelings I am experiencing or the person who these feelings are aimed at?

- When this heightened feeling subsides, what would make this person a good friend?

- What do we have in common? What hobbies and shared interests do we have?

- Do we share similar values about life?

- Do I trust this person?

If you find that your obsessive feelings or hyper-focus about a person is interfering with other areas of your life for a long period of time or making you unhappy, you will need to address this in the same way that you would any addictive behaviour. See **Chapter 7: Self-Care** for more on this.

More about ADHD and hypersensitivity

Hypersensitivity is not part of the diagnostic criteria for ADHD, but there is some evidence to suggest that hypersensitivity is common in people with ADHD. The physician Gabor Maté, who also has ADHD, believes that sensitivity is the root of ADD/ADHD. Some people with ADHD recognize that they have signs of hypersensitivity.

SO WHAT IS HYPERSENSITIVITY?

A hypersensitive or highly sensitive person may have a **greater awareness of sensory stimuli**, such as noise or smell or the texture of fabrics, and will find strong smells or bright lights uncomfortable. This is sometimes called **sensory-processing sensitivity**. A hypersensitive person will also experience emotional sensitivity and be more aware of the mood of the people around them and feel more sensitive to the comments or actions of others.

Activity for reflection

Are you a hypersensitive person? How many of the following statements resonate with you?

- **I am quick to notice subtle changes in the environment such as a slight change in someone's appearance.**

- **I can get overwhelmed in busy, noisy places.**

- **I am acutely aware of other people's facial expressions or tone of voice and can pick up on their moods easily.**

- **I find it easy to empathize when people feel sadness and I have a strong urge to comfort them.**

- **I am very scared of rejection and worry that people might not like me.**

- **I am sensitive to light, smell or sound, and external stimuli affect me more than other people.**

Hypersensitivity can be a beneficial quality, but self-care and self-esteem will help you manage some of the challenges, too.

Sensory-processing issues can also be a trait experienced by an autistic person.

Autism in girls can go undiagnosed as girls who are autistic can present differently.

If you think that you may be autistic – maybe you experience very heightened sensory-processing issues or find it challenging to navigate social situations – speak to your SENCO, parent/carer about why you feel that you could be autistic. See the back of this book for recommended reading to learn more about autism in girls.

End-of-chapter thoughts

- Is there anything that you have realized about yourself after reading this chapter? If so, what things have you learnt?

- In what ways do you think that ADHD affects your emotions and reactions? Is there any section in this chapter that you can particularly relate to? Which one?

- Can you think of some positive consequences of how you experience emotions? For example, do you think your sensitivity makes you more empathic towards others?

six

SELF-ESTEEM

*I*magine that one day, as you are waiting in a supermarket checkout queue, you overhear this conversation:

Person 1: **You are soo stupid! Who comes to the supermarket without their wallet? This is so typical of you.**

Person 2: Sorry, I forgot.

Person 1: **And why are you wearing those jeans? They look dreadful on you.**

Person 2: You are probably right. I won't wear them again.

Person 1: **Good...I mean someone like Sadie could get away with those jeans, but not you.**

Person 2:   OK.

Person 1:   **You just don't know how to dress – that is your problem.**

Listening to this conversation, you start to feel angry. You turn around to find out who is talking. You feel an overwhelming urge to say something and intervene.
   Should you:

- stare at person 1 to try to make them feel uncomfortable?

- say something nice to person 2, like 'Those jeans look great on you'?

- call out person 1 for what they are – a bully?

When we witness someone being treated badly or bullied, we recognize it's wrong. It might be really hard to stand by and not intervene.

Self-criticism

It can be hard to listen to a person being criticized and shamed, but the thoughts we have about ourselves – **the internal voice in our minds – can also become very negative**.

Activity for reflection

- Do you think that you are **often self-critical**? What kind of thoughts do you have about yourself when you are feeling low?

- Do you **encourage yourself to try new things** or put yourself down and avoid new experiences?

- Is your internal monologue often **negative and self-limiting**?

- Do you make **negative generalizations** about yourself after one incident? For example: 'Jo shouted at me because I am annoying', 'I did not pass the test because I am stupid.'

- Do you constantly **compare yourself to others**?

What do you think your answers tell you about your self-esteem?

Self-esteem and ADHD

Self-esteem – **how we perceive ourselves** – begins to develop in early infancy and is shaped by the messages we receive about ourselves from family, peers, teachers and even the media.

Growing up with ADHD, you may have been told off or criticized for behaviour you found hard to control. Comments such as 'you are annoying' or 'you are lazy' or 'you never try hard enough' can be internalized and result in feelings of inadequacy.

Perhaps you felt that you needed to change something about yourself to be more acceptable to others?

If your internal self-talk is often negative, you will seek the approval of others to bolster your self-esteem. You may try to mould yourself into the kind of person you think others would like.

Many girls with ADHD try hard to conceal or hide traits about themselves that they think will prompt negative feedback.

Contingent self-esteem

It is natural to feel pride when you accomplish a goal or achieve something that you worked hard at. Who is not boosted by praise or a compliment?

"Your drawing is great!"
"That jacket suits you."
"I admire your determination."

Positive comments like this can boost our mood. But the fleeting sense of pride we feel when we have achieved something or earned praise from others should not be confused with true self-esteem. True self-esteem is **a general feeling that you are enough**.

If your self-esteem is insecure, you may strive to gain the admiration of others to feel validated. If you rely on external validation or try to meet external standards to feel better about yourself, your self-esteem will fluctuate very easily.

 "I aced my English exam, so I must be OK."

Self-esteem goes up.

 "My results in the English exam are not as good as I hoped or as good as…"

Self-esteem goes down.

CONTINGENT SELF-ESTEEM IS FRAGILE

When your self-esteem is contingent, you may also avoid challenging yourself. Failure can be extremely painful if your sense of self-worth hinges on success. You may play it safe in your personal or academic or professional life to avoid the risk of disappointment, but in doing so, you limit your experiences and opportunities to learn.

Activity for reflection

- Do you work hard to prove yourself to other people at school or work?

- Do you find it hard to ask for help from others, preferring to show that you have things 'under control'?

- Are you very hard on yourself in a particular area, such as schoolwork or your appearance?

- Are you a perfectionist?

- Are you a people pleaser? Do you try hard to be liked by others?

If you answered YES to several of the questions above, you will need to take the steps below to gradually shift away from contingent self-esteem.

The pillars of true self-esteem

A person with good self-esteem does not need to be the best at something to feel worthy. They are kind and compassionate towards themselves. They are their own best friends. Let us think about what we mean by a 'good friend'. Would you add anything to this list below?

A **good friend** is:

- someone who **you enjoy spending time with**

- **positive and encouraging** towards you

- a person who **accepts you as you are**

- **kind** to you

- **honest** with you

- likely to try to persuade you to do **what is right for you**.

If you have low or insecure self-esteem, you will need to unlearn some habits and patterns of self-criticism. This will not be easy. It will take patience and work over years. The effort is worth it, though. Healthy self-esteem enables you to **bounce back from disappointment** more easily, to challenge yourself in life and to enjoy your own company.

Six ways to develop true self-esteem

1. SET YOURSELF GOALS THAT ARE NOT ACHIEVEMENT-BASED

It is good to set yourself goals and to have a purpose, but your goals should be based on **long-term aims** that allow you to enjoy learning more about a subject or area of interest or to learn more about yourself.

Activity for reflection

Write down two or three goals that are not achievement-based. In other words, you cannot measure the result from completion or grades or positive feedback from others. Instead, **your aim is to experience the process of working towards these goals over the next two or three years.**
For example:

- I would like to learn to dance salsa.

- I would like to learn to feel more confident when I meet new people.

- I would like to volunteer to work with animals.

- I would like to become less anxious.

2. FIND CREATIVE PURSUITS AND INTERESTS

Creative and active pursuits are vital when you have ADHD – they enable you to **channel your mental energy into something rewarding**, which allows less time for you to sit and ruminate.

You may already have a few hobbies or interests that you enjoy. If you don't, it's time to start exploring things that you might like to pursue.

Activity for reflection

Read through each of these statements below and tick the ones that apply to you. You can tick as many or as few as you like.

1. I like to make things and do practical tasks.

2. I like art and have always drawn or been interested in creating pieces of art.

3. I like writing or creating stories.

4. I like drama and communicating to people.

5. I am very musical and can sing or play music or make music.

6. I like figuring out how things work.

7. I am very curious about how people's minds work and about psychology.

8. I am a very sporty person and love incorporating movement into my everyday life.

9. I like thinking about philosophical questions and how we live our life.

10. I love helping people and improving their lives in some way.

Now think about what activities you could try out that involve these skills.

For example, if you picked 4 and 7, why not join a local amateur dramatic club and find out if there is a free online psychology course you could try?

When you actively pursue an interest, your strengths and talents can often reveal themselves. Remember, most of us don't have strengths that are instantly recognizable – a fast runner is easy to identify in races, but generally we discover our strengths gradually as we develop an area of skill from pursuing our interests.

3. CHALLENGE NEGATIVE SELF-TALK

If your friend always seems to lose their keys, you might make a little joke and help them look for them, but you certainly wouldn't see it as a sign of something essentially faulty with your friend.

Negative self-talk involves lots of generalized thinking. If you get a lower test grade than you wanted, you might think, 'Typical. I am useless.'

You were a bit nervous giving a speech in class, you might think, 'I just embarrassed myself. I can't do public speaking. I am a joke.'

Negative self-talk is pretty harsh, isn't it? Almost **abusive**. If you heard somebody talking to friend like that, you would probably call them out on it. **Negative self-talk is an example of cognitive distortion. Your thinking will convince you that something is true.**

Recognize the patterns you follow when you engage in negative self-talk and actively try to counter it by saying what a good friend would.

Counter a negative generalization with a specific comment and a positive comment. If you think:

I should have known I would do badly. I am just dumb.

Counter that thought immediately:

You knew that maths is not your favourite subject (specific comment).

You actually did a lot better than last time (positive comment).

Think about a time when you were very negative towards yourself. What could you say differently to yourself?

4. RECOGNIZE THE DIFFERENCE BETWEEN CONSTRUCTIVE CRITICISM AND NEGATIVE CRITICISM

Constructive criticism helps us improve and learn. This type of criticism is specific and gives you realistic and achievable tips to improve.

Example of constructive criticism from an English teacher:

Try changing the first sentence to include more description.

Negative criticism is intended to hurt us. When people give negative criticism, they are often angry, unhappy or may have low self-esteem themselves. They may feel that putting someone else down will help them feel better about themselves. What they say is not a truth and is often a blanket opinion.

5. FIND ROLE MODELS WHO REPRESENT DIVERSE AND NON-CONFORMING IDEALS

Follow people on social media who inspire you to be brave and unique. People who embody body positivity and who are not afraid to be individual will spread messages that encourage others to challenge negative stereotypes and reductive ideas in society.

　　Remember, that there are many residual ideals around beauty standards and behaviour expectation that perpetuate racist, sexist or homophobic ideas. For example, the idea that every female body should look a certain way.

> **Empower yourself to recognize messages in the media that do not encourage us to value ourselves but instead tap into insecurities to sell products or services.**
>
> **You may feel worse about yourself after reading a magazine or looking through someone's feed on social media, whereas another article or social media account uplifts you.**

6. DRESS FOR YOURSELF

Wear make-up **when and if you feel like it. You are not obliged to be decorative for anyone else or to always 'look your best'.** Sometimes, people 'hide' behind make-up or clothes due to insecurity. Dressing up should be enjoyable and **on your terms** and not out of a sense of shame or obligation.

End-of-chapter thoughts

- In what ways do you think that your self-esteem is contingent?

- What do you think you do currently to gain the approval of others?

- What can you do differently to avoid seeking the validation of others to feel good about yourself?

- What steps will you take first to improve your self-esteem?

seven

SELF-CARE

*Y*ou buy two pot plants and place them on a bookshelf in your bedroom. You look after both plants in **exactly the same way**. After several weeks, **one of the plants has thrived while the other plant has withered – its leaves have turned yellow and shrivelled**.

You assume the plant is dead and throw it out. As you do, you spot the care label on the underside of the pot. It reads:

This plant needs plenty of sunshine.

You pick it out of the trash and move the plant to the sunniest room.

Two weeks later, the plant has doubled in size and small purple flowers have sprouted on its stem.

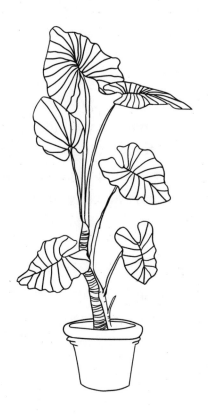

Just like plants, we humans each need particular conditions to thrive. The **right environment** can make the difference between thriving and evolving or struggling and stagnating.

Sometimes society can make us feel as if we are all expected to behave in the same way and like the same things. The truth is that as a neurodivergent individual, you will only thrive in an environment that is right for you.

"I did work experience in an office when I was in Year 10 (US Grade 9). My friend found it quite enjoyable and was able to keep up with the admin tasks, whereas I hated every second of it. Not talking to anyone for hours and processing data nearly drove me to tears. Also, because the work was so boring, I kept making simple mistakes and the boss looked irritated with me."

When you have ADHD, it is even more important to think deeply about what you need in your life to thrive. You need to develop an understanding of what your interests are, what kind of company helps you feel comfortable in yourself and what support and environment suits you the best.

School can feel like a one-size-fits-all place where you have to try to fit in, but in school the right adaptations, accommodations and support can make a massive difference.

Developing self knowledge is a personal and individual journey, yet there are definitely core non-negotiable self-care tips for anyone with ADHD.

Self-care non-negotiables for anyone with ADHD

1. SPEND MOST OF YOUR TIME WITH PEOPLE WHO ENERGIZE YOU

When you have ADHD, it is important to spend most of your time with people who like you for who you are, who 'get you' and who understand and appreciate you. The positivity you feel about yourself when you are with these people will energize you. **Whether it be family or a good friend or mentor, one person like this in your life is more beneficial than 20 friends who you are not comfortable around.** Too often we accept friendships that leave us feeling depleted or dissatisfied, so that we are not 'alone', but who you spend free time with can have a massive impact on your well-being.

Activity for reflection

Think about all the friends and workmates you spend the most time with and ask yourself these three important questions:

- When I am with this person, **do I feel good about myself most of the time**?

- After I have spent time with this person, do I generally feel **more energized and positive** than before or do I very often feel that I might have done or said something wrong?

- Do I feel that **this person enjoys my company** or do I feel as if I need to try hard with them?

If you have answered NO to two or more, then the company of this person is draining rather than energizing you. So, what do you do?

Friends we don't always 'click with'

When you spend time with a person who is very different to you, you may occasionally feel unsure that you are doing or saying the 'right thing'. **Spending time with people who are different to you can be incredibly positive, as long as you both feel respected and valued.** If you get a feeling that someone is picking at you or sometimes makes you feel bad, trust your instincts on this, but also follow this up by speaking to them in a non-confrontational way, if possible.

What should you do when a 'friend' makes you feel bad about yourself?

You may have a friend who is always making little digs at you, such as 'You are so clumsy!' or 'You are so ditzy!' They'd pass it off as a joke, but the 'drip, drip' effect of these comments will affect your self-confidence.

Calmly explain that you would like the comments to stop because you feel undermined by them. How your friend responds to this will give you some idea about whether you can move forward. If they respect your boundaries, the discussion was useful and you can both learn and grow from each other. If they do not take your comments on board or accuse you of being too sensitive, then reconsider spending time with them.

2. REGULAR MOVEMENT/EXERCISE

There is plenty of evidence to suggest that exercise and physical movement are one of the most effective ways of managing ADHD.

Exercise increases the blood flow to all areas of the brain. Increased blood flow to the front of the brain

and the pre-frontal cortex can improve concentration and attention.

Exercise also affects the release of neurotransmitters, such as dopamine, which are typically produced at lower levels in people with ADHD. Raised dopamine levels will also improve your attention and motivation.

Have you found that after physical exercise, it was easier to settle down to a task that you were putting off before?

We all know the benefits of exercise, so what might stop us from doing it?

If you think of exercise as another chore, this will seriously deter you. Exercise does not need to include going to a gym class or running. Exercise is movement. Any movement that raises your heart beat a little.

This could be brisk walking, dancing, riding a bike, climbing, swimming, or even going up lots of flights of stairs.

- **Swap the 'all or nothing' for 'something is better than nothing' approach.**

- **Make the preparation stage before a task easier.**

Very often, it is not task itself that is off-putting, but the preparation you need to do beforehand that puts you off. For example, you want to exercise, but the idea of finding your gym gear, getting dressed and getting to the gym seems like an impossible mountain to climb. Create easy access and a **minimum-fuss approach** to tasks.

Tips to increase your access to exercise

- Keep lots of spare gym clothes in a separate box or cupboard, so you don't have to search for clean clothes.

- Find ways of exercising that is easy to get to – the swanky gym that is a bus ride away may be a less sensible option than the smaller gym around the corner.

- Walk to places when you can and vary your way of travelling. Try cycling or rollerblading to places.

3. FIND A CREATIVE OUTLET

Girls with ADHD have busy brains, minds that are always searching for stimulation. If there is no alternative, a mind in search of stimulation will engage in worry or rumination.

A creative outlet is important because it distracts you and can bring you out of a negative loop of thinking. Even if you feel tired or down and are tempted to not do your favourite activities, try as much as you can to keep going.

4. CHOOSE WORK OR A SUBJECT TO STUDY THAT IS INTERESTING MOST OF THE TIME

When you are at school, you don't get a lot of choice about what to study. But it is really good to start thinking early about what subjects and activities you enjoy the most. **When you leave school or college, any further study, training or work you do should be interesting to you most of the time.**

(No course or job in the world is completely without some boring tasks.)

Activity for reflection

If you are making choices about what to study at college or what lines of work you might pursue, consider which of these statements sound like you:

When I am at work or studying this subject...

- **I can sometimes get 'in the zone' and become focused and fully engaged in what I am doing.**

- **I often use my strengths and skills.**

- **I often feel that I am getting better with time.**

- **I often get ideas about how to improve things.**

Did you answer NO to three or more of the statements?

If you picked to study a course and are not enjoying it, speak to your course tutor or someone you trust about this.

If the course you study is compulsory, speak to your teacher and tutor to explain to them what is hard. They can support you better if they know what is difficult for you and make adaptations to the study programme or teaching methods, so that you can do better.

Learn healthy coping mechanisms

When you have ADHD, you spend most of your time actively seeking out mental stimulation. This could be in the form of work, mind wandering, daydreaming or taking on numerous new projects. **You may thrive for a while, but you will eventually become overstimulated and feel frazzled. In this state of exhaustion, rather than relax and sleep more, you may actually find it harder to unwind.**

During this time of mental exhaustion, you may:

- find it harder than usual to regulate your attention and flit around from one activity to another

- feel disconnected from your core emotions and thoughts

- eat mindlessly or spend hours staring at your phone or engage in more unhealthy sensation-seeking activities, such as online shopping.

If you do not find a way to recalibrate your mind and body, these feelings can spiral and leave you more vulnerable to anxiety or low mood.

Self-care involves recognizing when your mind or body needs to slow down and become centred again.

Sitting at home in bed will not necessarily help you feel better, especially if you still have access to technology. Instead, try some of these strategies:

1. VISIT AND SPEND TIME IN NATURE

If your mind is whirring, go to the coast or spend time by a lake or in a forest. **The sensory experience of being in nature will help open you up to the external world in a way that calm and soothe a busy mind.** Whether it be listening to the waves crashing against the sand or feeling the breeze against your skin, the natural world can help awaken a part of us that becomes shut off when we are anxious or stressed.

2. TAKE MENTAL HEALTH DAYS OFF AND/OR SLOW DOWN

When we feel physically sick, we gauge how bad it is and we may decide to take some time off, to get better. The only way you can recover or heal is to **slow down** to give your body a chance to repair itself. This approach should be the same if we notice signs that our mental health is beginning to suffer. **Your brain will often send clear signs of this because your thought patterns will become more repetitive and negative.**

3. TAKE A DAY TRIP SOMEWHERE NEW AND VISIT NEW PLACES

Visiting a new destination can awaken your senses and bring you out of a rut, especially if you feel uninspired by your daily routine or find that your daily life is causing you

to over-worry. Try to explore new places, even if it's only somewhere new in your city or town.

4. DO FUN THINGS THAT HELP YOU STAY 'PRESENT'

Any activity as simple as riding a bike down a hill or going to a funfair, goofing around with friends or playing cards can help you feel **relaxed and more present**. Write down at least five simple activities that you like to do to relax or enjoy. **Prioritize activities that don't result in hyper-focus, but help you engage with the world externally and mindfully.** You won't suddenly feel better from participating in one activity, so continue to do this every day to re-adjust your internal thermostat from stressed to less stressed.

5. MEDITATION

This may seem like **a big ask**, but it is possible to meditate when you have ADHD.

The following article gives some tips on how to meditate

with ADHD and how meditation can help you relax, when you have ADHD.

www.additudemag.com/how-to-meditate-for-adhd-symptoms

6. LISTEN TO AN AUDIO BOOK

When you are anxious and your brain is tired, it can be hard to settle to reading, but **listening to an audio book demands less conscious effort and allows you to ground yourself by listening to the spoken words.**

7. WATCH A FAVOURITE FILM/TV PROGRAMME

Any film that will make you laugh – stay away from disaster movies for a while – can lift your mood. **Watch a comedy and allow yourself to laugh.**

8. WRITE ABOUT YOUR DAY IN A DIARY OR JOURNAL

Writing or recording your thoughts can help you untangle them and crystalize or renew your sense of purpose. In times of stress, writing down your thoughts may help you identify any practical steps you can take to handle any current challenges.

Sleep and ADHD

There is nothing more frustrating than feeling tired all day, only to feel **wide awake at night. Night-time is often when you are tempted to engage in self-directed activities that you want to do, even if you are tired.** The demands of school or work have finished and you may see this as an opportunity to go on your phone, watch TV or play a video game – all of which increase your exposure to blue light. The more overstimulated and tired you are, the less likely it is that you will sleep well.

When you have ADHD, you may have a delayed sleep cycle and naturally fall asleep later.

There is no hard and fast rule to aid sleep. **It may be useful to accept that your sleep will be occasionally disrupted, but if your sleep cycle has become disrupted over a few days or longer, you may need to look at what**

you are doing during the day, not just what you do before bed.

Try some of these strategies:

- **Tire your body out** with more movement and increase your intake of fresh air.

- **Ensure that the day includes a balance of activities** and that you have done something you enjoy.

- **Try to have a time when you switch off devices** (easier said than done).

If sleeplessness becomes very frequent, speak to a doctor.

Unhealthy coping mechanisms

Coping mechanisms are strategies you use to help you manage challenging times. We all use coping mechanisms in our lives, but some of coping mechanisms may be unhealthy. **Unhealthy coping mechanisms usually bring short-term relief, but will cause long-term problems. If you rely on the following unhealthy coping mechanisms, you may experience difficulties in multiple areas of your life.**

1. USING ANXIETY TO FUEL PRODUCTIVITY

Functioning anxiety is a very common coping mechanism and is one reason why many girls with ADHD do not show

obvious signs of ADHD. They may be using anxiety to juggle demands of school or work and to cover up weaknesses of executive function.

 "I constantly felt like I was juggling balls to keep up. I did well at school, but I did not sleep properly or have time to do anything else because I had to spend so much of my free time to keep up with work."

The problem with existing in a state of functioning anxiety is that it will exhaust you eventually. Some level of stress can be beneficial to us, as long as we feel also have **time to recoup and rest**. If our life is constantly lived under a certain level of stress, then it is unhealthy. If you find that you are living under continuous stress,  consider seeking a **coach or mentor** who can help you decide how to balance the activities for the week and **prioritize what to do**. It's perfectly OK to get support on this.

2. PLEASURE-SEEKING ACTIVITIES CAN BECOME ADDICTIVE

Pleasure-seeking is any activity that helps you **feel good in the short term**. This could be eating chocolate or playing video games or binging on junk food. Everyone indulges in pleasure-seeking behaviour from time to time. It's a **part of the human experience. But pleasure seeking can become a**

crutch that we rely on to feel better or to feel stimulated.
When any pleasure-seeking activity becomes a coping
mechanism, then there is a risk of becoming addicted.

**Pleasure-seeking behaviours that can become
addictive include:**

- **binge eating**

- **overspending money**

- **gambling**

- **obsessive use of social media**

- **abusing substances such as alcohol**

- **maladaptive daydreaming (see Chapter 4: Your
  Wandering Mind).**

People often associate the word **addiction** with serious
substance abuse or alcoholism, but it can include even **very
familiar activities; there is a higher incidence of binge-
eating disorder among people with ADHD than those
without ADHD.** Binge eating – craving and eating excessive
amounts of food in a very short space of time – could easily
be dismissed as less serious than some other addictions, but
it can lead to serious health risks.

**The most important first step to dealing with any
addiction is to recognize it.** If you can recognize that you
may be addicted to something, then you will be able to take
the next step.

Activity for reflection

Are you showing signs of addictive behaviour? How many of the following questions would you answer YES?

- **Do I spend the majority of my time engaging in the behaviour or thinking about it?**

- **Do I continue with this behaviour even if I know it is resulting in physical and mental harm?**

- **Do I have trouble stopping this behaviour?**

- **Do I use this behaviour as a coping mechanism when I feel down or worried?**

- **Am I often tuning out of other areas of my life to indulge in this behaviour?**

- **Do I feel really irritable when I try to stop this behaviour?**

You are far more likely to indulge in addictive behaviours if you are feeling stressed, over-tired, anxious or depressed, so addressing these other areas of your life is important.

Are you 'mental health aware'?

We are taught early on that if we feel very ill, we should go to the doctor. **If you broke a bone, you would not think twice about seeking immediate medical attention. Yet people often wait a too long before seeking support for mental ill health.** The principle is the same – the earlier you seek help and advice, the quicker you can help yourself recover.

If you feel that your thoughts of anxiety and low mood have been going on for longer than two weeks and are not improving, take these steps:

- Speak to a doctor or school counsellor. When we experience persistent feelings of anxiety worry or persistent low mood, we may need additional support to get better.

- The most common mental health illnesses are anxiety, depression and post-traumatic stress disorder. If you feel you may be experiencing any of these, read the links below to learn more about what you can do and what treatment is available.

Anxiety

The NHS website provides some useful information about anxiety. Follow the link below where you will find really useful information about anxiety and panic attacks. This includes:

- A list of **dos and don'ts** of what to do if you are experiencing a panic attack or feelings of anxiety.

- Information about the **signs and symptoms** of anxiety and panic attacks.

- A link to a **mood self-assessment** to find out if you have symptoms of anxiety and are experiencing panic attacks.

- An audio guide to help you **manage feelings of panic or anxiety**.

  www.nhs.uk/conditions/stress-anxiety-depression/understanding-panic

The doctor may suggest some types of therapy such as CBT (cognitive behavioural therapy) to manage obsessive thinking and anxiety.

TIPS TO HELP YOU MANAGE FEELINGS OF PANIC

If you experience feelings of panic, some breathing techniques can help you calm these feelings down.

Make yourself as comfortable as you can. If you can, loosen any clothes that restrict your breathing.

If you're lying down, place your arms a little bit away from your sides, with the palms up. Let your legs be straight, or bend your knees so your feet are flat on the floor.

If you're sitting, place your arms on the chair arms.

If you're sitting or standing, place both feet flat on the ground. Whatever position you're in, place your feet roughly hip-width apart.

- **Let your breath flow as deep down into your belly as is comfortable, without forcing it.**
- **Try breathing in through your nose and out through your mouth.**
- **Breathe in gently and regularly. Some people find it helpful to count steadily from 1 to 5. You may not be able to reach 5 at first.**
- **Then, without pausing or holding your breath, let it flow out gently, counting from 1 to 5 again, if you find this helpful.**
- **Keep doing this for 3 to 5 minutes.**

www.nhs.uk/conditions/stress-anxiety-depression/ ways-relieve-stress

GROUNDING YOURSELF

When you experience physical symptoms of anxiety, **grounding techniques** can help you to recentre.

Try as many of the following exercises as you can to help bring your thoughts back to the present and calm feelings of panic:

- **What can you hear?** Listen carefully to any sounds you can hear. Can you identify three different sounds? Listen carefully to each sound for five seconds.

- **What can you feel?** Touch or pick up three different things. For example, you might grab an ice cube from your drink and hold it for a few seconds, or stroke the fabric on the chair you are sitting on. Focus on how each item feels against your skin.

- **What can you see?** Look around you. Focus on three things that you can see. Focus on the colour, texture, and movement of what you are looking at for five seconds.

- **What can you smell?** Try to focus on what you can smell. Pick up three items around you, such as a bottle of juice or a jumper, and smell each one for a few seconds.

Trauma and ADHD

If you have experienced a traumatic event or events in your past, such as bullying, abuse, family dysfunction or the death of a close relative, this may still be affecting you. **Post-traumatic stress disorder is more common than most people think and describes the long-term effects of a past traumatic experience.**

Follow this link to learn more about post-traumatic stress disorder:

https://youngminds.org.uk/find-help/conditions/ptsd

Depression

Around 300 million people a year experience depression. It is extremely common, but the early signs are often ignored. **Remember that you may be functionally depressed and still manage to go to school or college, but this does not mean that you should not seek help.** In actual fact, seeking help early is preferable. Follow these links to learn more about depression:

https://youngminds.org.uk/find-help/conditions/ depression

www.nhs.uk/mental-health/conditions/clinical-depression/overview

End-of-chapter thoughts

- What self-care practices would you like to incorporate into your life?

- Do you feel that you need additional support to help you with your mental health? What is the first step to access that support and who can help you to access that support?

eight

LIFE AFTER SCHOOL

After leaving school and college I found it really hard to organize myself into action. I worried that I would never achieve anything. I had all these dreams and ideas, but I did not know how to implement them. I was frozen by indecision.

When you are younger, everything seems so much simpler – we often believe that things will comfortably slot into place. The reality is the next few years can be humbling and daunting.

Common stumbling blocks after school

You might have spent months dreaming about the day you would finally be free from the **constraints and restrictions of school life** – free to begin a chapter of greater personal freedom when you can become who you really want to be and follow your dreams. After a while, though, you may come across a few of these stumbling blocks that throw you off course:

YOU RE-EVALUATE ALL YOUR CHILDHOOD DREAMS

When you were a younger, you may have thought you had a clear idea of what you wanted to do with your life. **Children sometimes fixate on jobs that they think will bring fame and adulation, such as a singer or sports star.** Dreams you had as a child are a projection of a desire, an impression of a feeling you are chasing.

Moving from adolescence to adulthood, you will get a better understanding of the reality of jobs and of who you are. You may even discard or renew childhood goals and ideals. This time of reflection can be painful and daunting as you will need to begin again to think about the direction you want to take in education or training.

YOU MIGHT MISS THE STRUCTURE OF SCHOOL!

This may seem hard to believe, but **school provided a framework and structure to your day. Without that structure, it can be easier to get sidetracked by tempting distractions** – who is to stop you playing video games all day, every day? This easy access to appealing distractions can throw you off track and leave you feeling constantly disappointed in yourself.

You may have lots of dreams and ideas about what to do, but it can be hard to plot your next step and follow through on goals.

YOU MIGHT BE FROZEN BY CHOICES AND DECISIONS

You may feel an overwhelming pressure to suddenly have **answers to big questions** like **'What do I want to do with my life?', 'What career path should I follow?',** 'What are my goals?' and become frozen with fear about making the wrong choices.

YOU MAY START COMPARING YOURSELF WITH OTHERS

You will start to compare yourself with others who seem to know what they are doing, further intensifying your sense of fear about what to do next.

The value of the journey

The years beyond school are so much more than slotting into a career or job; they are for learning more about what is important to you and how you want to live. This involves trial and error, disappointments and successes over time.

Here are five top tips to help you navigate this journey ahead:

1. PRIORITIZE YOUR MENTAL HEALTH

As well as learning about your goals and career, you will gain further information about what you need in your life to enjoy better mental health. This is more valuable than chasing a career. **Building a solid emotional foundation will help you better understand who you are and what you truly want to do rather than blindly following a direction you think that you should.**

2. DON'T FOCUS ON CHASING DREAMS – FOCUS ON COMPLETING ACTIONS

Many people with ADHD find it easier to manage their time when they have some clarity about the direction they are moving in and what they are working towards. Imagine you are in a small boat out at sea. Without any oars, you would not really go anywhere, but drift about aimlessly. When you have oars, you can control what direction that you want to go in

Set yourself concrete achievable goals that allow you to move forward in a general direction of where you want to go.

Example:

"I am interested in film so think that I might like to pursue film direction." (Sam, 18)

"I will study a film course at college (= achievable goal)."

The goal is achievable in the near future and it provides Sam with a clear next step. Working towards this achievable goal will provide Sam with useful experience and knowledge that could help her achieve her dream or to learn about the area she is interested in.

Even if Sam decides that film directing is not for her, she has learnt about an area of interest that will inform her next decision, bringing her closer to a better understanding of what she wants. She is **moving forward with a sense of purpose**.

3. IDENTIFY CLEAR ACTIONS FOR THE NEXT YEAR OR TWO

Think about actions that you can take in the next year or two that could help you develop your knowledge in an area that you are interested in. Keep your number of actions very low. If you have written too many, it could be difficult to plan for and achieve these goals. If you have no more than two, it will be much easier to take the necessary steps to achieve the goal.

Write out two goals for the next 1–2 years

The purpose of identifying clear goals is that this will help give you a sense of direction and purpose. One goal should be personal and one should be career/work-based.

> Example: 'Goals – I want to apply to do a degree in Fashion and Design and I want to feel more confident about myself.'

Explore how and why you want to achieve each goal

Goal	Why	How	When	Plan
To apply for a Foundation Degree in Art.	This course is based around my interest in art. The course includes a module on comic illustration, which I am interested in.	I will complete my portfolio and ask my Art teacher to write a statement for me.	The deadline is…	Complete two pictures for my portfolio. Ask Ms Jones for her input. Speak to my English teacher to check my statement on the application form.

Identify the actions you need to complete to meet the goal

Under each goal, write down all the steps you need to take to achieve the goal, in any order:

Goal: I want to apply to do a degree in Fashion and Design.

I need to:

- Meet the application deadline on…

- I need to submit a portfolio by…

- I need to have more drawings in my portfolio.

- I need to work on three pieces by…and do a new piece every two weeks.

- My Art teacher will give me advice and tips.

- I need to write a personal statement. My English teacher will help me formulate ideas.

Map out your action plan on a calendar

Follow the same steps now as described in **Chapter 2: Executive Functioning and ADHD** for working to deadlines. Remember with any action plan you will need to:

- **Review and adapt your action plans regularly.** An action plan is not set in stone. Think of your action plan as a living, breathing thing that changes and evolves with time. An action plan provides a framework and a sense of direction. There should be space to manoeuvre.

- **Be prepared to shift some deadlines around sometimes.** Recognize that you will have days when you are very productive and days when you are less productive. Allow yourself this time.

- **Every few weeks or months, make small changes to your action plan so that is interesting and achievable.**

4. GET ADVICE ABOUT MONEY MATTERS

It would be wrong to ignore the fact that your individual circumstances play a role in how hard or easy it is to access certain services or opportunities. Internships can be useful experience, but many young people cannot afford to work for no pay. Many young people have to juggle the demands of study with part-time work, which requires much more planning and organization of your time.

Seek support and advice

- There are various support networks available that can advise you about student finances and support. **Ask to speak to student finance support services before applying to do any further study at a college or university; they can advise you on your financial options.**

- **There are also apprenticeships or subsidized training routes into careers that you may be interested in.** Many large companies or organizations have entry-level training schemes that are subsidized. **This is often listed under career opportunities on the company website.**

5. EAT AS HEALTHILY AS YOU CAN, MOST OF THE TIME

With increased independence comes responsibility.
We have all heard this at one time or another in our

lives. **But when you experience challenges with executive function, these 'responsibilities' for looking after yourself can be overwhelming.** If you have moved out of home to start college or university, you will need to do your own shopping, cooking, cleaning and laundry.

Many people with ADHD may rely increasingly on junk food or processed food for convenience and to avoid the additional chores of shopping and cooking. This is understandable, but eating badly will affect your mental health and exacerbate challenges with ADHD drastically.

Find easy approaches to healthy eating

Cooking can take a long time and requires **organization, concentration and focus**. There may be times when your focus is somewhere else and you cannot suddenly switch your attention to making a nutritious meal. **You will  wait and get hungrier and hungrier and then raid the cupboard to find a bag of crisps or chocolate bar to settle your hunger. No nutrition whatsoever.**

Five-minute recipes

Cooking a very quick meal is preferable to raiding the cupboard for junk food.

The British Heart Foundation has a lot of recipes that only take five minutes to prepare. Follow this link to learn more:

www.bhf.org.uk/informationsupport/heart-matters-magazine/nutrition/cooking-skills/quick-healthy-meals

Stock up on foods that need no cooking

It is useful to have a supply of **healthy, easy-to-prepare food** that require no cooking for these situations:

Choose three from this list and have a snack plate:

- tins of ready cooked chickpeas, beans, vegetables, baked beans
- carrots
- tomatoes
- celery sticks
- tins of canned fish
- slices of cheese or cooked turkey or chicken slices
- rye bread
- fortified breakfast cereals
- nuts
- fruit
- cheese
- yoghurts.

End-of-chapter thoughts

- Have you identified any actions you would like to take in the next year or two? If so, what are these actions?

- What would you like to feel about yourself in the next year or two?

- What do you think are the greatest obstacles you face in meeting your goals for the next year? Can you think of anyone who can offer advice and guidance to help you meet these goals?

6—12 months later

RE-EVALUATING YOUR SELF KNOWLEDGE

In each chapter of this book there are activities for reflection and at the end of each chapter some things to think about.

Skim through these questions again after six months. Experiences that you continue to have will provide you with even more knowledge about yourself.

Add any further ideas, strategies or thoughts that you have below each heading.

Attention regulation (Chapter 1)

What strategies have helped you the most with attention regulation?

....

....

....

....

....

....

Executive functioning (Chapter 2)

Have you found any approaches that help you navigate some of your challenges with executive functioning?

....

....

....

....

....

Have you found that you are better at managing any of these areas:

- meeting study deadlines

- timekeeping

- finding or not losing things

- keeping things organized?

. . . .

. . . .

. . . .

. . . .

. . . .

. . . .

Which area of executive functioning do you need more support with?

. . . .

. . . .

. . . .

ADHD strengths (Chapter 3)

What strengths have you explored and developed? How do you think you maximize your strengths day to day?

. . . .

. . . .

. . . .

Mind wandering (Chapter 4)

Are you more aware of what your mind is doing when it wanders? How has this awareness helped you?

. . . .

. . . .

. . . .

What do you do to try to control some of the pitfalls of mind wandering?

. . . .

. . . .

. . . .

Emotions (Chapter 5)

Is there anything different that you do to try to manage strong emotions, especially anger?

. . . .

. . . .

. . . .

Do you feel that you have a better understanding of what situations trigger the strongest feelings of anger and rejection? Do you think you understand why?

. . . .

. . . .

. . . .

Self-esteem (Chapter 6)

How have you tried to develop true self-esteem?

. . . .

. . . .

. . . .

Do you think that you still seek external validation to feel better about yourself? In what ways do you still do that?

. . . .

. . . .

. . . .

Self-care (Chapter 7)

What do you do in your life that is self-care?

. . . .

. . . .

. . . .

Do you think that you could improve in any area of self-care? Which area would you like to focus on?

. . . .

. . . .

. . . .

References

Aron, E.N. (2003) *The Highly Sensitive Person: How to Thrive When the World Overwhelms You.* London: Thorsons Classics Edition.

Glaser Holthe, M.E. and Langvik, E. (2017) 'The strives, struggles, and successes of women diagnosed with ADHD as adults.' *SAGE Open 7*, 1. doi: 10.1177/2158244017701799doi: 10.1177/2158244017701799.

Griffin, M.J. (n.d.) 'Do boys and girls show the same signs of ADHD?' Accessed on 14/05/2021 at www.understood.org/en/learning-thinking-differences/child-learning-disabilities/add-adhd/do-boys-and-girls-show-same-adhd-symptoms.

Halevy-Yosef, R., Bachar, E., Shaley, L., Pollak, Y. *et al.* (2019) 'The complexity of the interaction between binge-eating and attention.' *PLoS One 14*, 4, e0215506.

Hoogman, M., Stolte, M., Bass, M. and Kroesbergern, E. (2020) 'Creativity and ADHD: A review of behavioral studies, the effect of psychostimulants and neural underpinnings.' *Neuroscience & Biobehavioral Reviews 119*, 66–85.

Maté, G. (1999) *Scattered Minds: The Origins and Healing of Attention Deficit Disorder.* London: Penguin Random House.

Panagiotidi, M., Overton, P.G. and Stafford, T. (2020) 'The relationship between sensory processing sensitivity and attention deficit hyperactivity disorder traits: A spectrum approach.' *Psychiatry Research 293*, 113477. doi: 10.1016/j.psychres.2020.113477.

Park, S. (2019) '11 Bad*ss women who are thriving with ADHD.' Popsugar. Accessed on 02/06/2021 at www.popsugar.co.uk/fitness/Famous-Women-ADHD-46158675?utm_medium=redirect&utm_campaign=US:GB&utm_source=www.bing.com.

Soates, L.S., de Souza Costa, D., Malloy-Diniz, L.F., Romano-Silva, M.A., de Paula, J.J. and de Miranda, D.M. (2019) 'Investigation on the attention deficit hyperactivity disorder effect on infatuation and impulsivity in adolescents.' *Behavioral Neuroscience*. doi: 10.3389/fnbeh.2019.00137.

Understood Team (n.d.) 'Celebrity Spotlight: Why will.i.am says ADHD fuels his creativity.' Understood for All. Accessed on 02/06/2021 at www.understood.org/en/learning-thinking-differences/personal-stories/famous-people/celebrity-spotlight-why-william-says-adhd-fuels-his-creativity.

White, H. (2019) 'The creativity of ADHD.' *Scientific American*. Accessed on 14/05/2021 at www.scientificamerican.com/article/the-creativity-of-adhd.

Young, S., Adamo, N., Ásgeirsdóttir, B.B., Branney, P. *et al.* (2020) 'Females with ADHD: An expert consensus statement taking a lifespan approach providing guidance for the identification and treatment of attention-deficit/hyperactivity disorder in girls and women.' *BMC Psychiatry 20*, 404. doi: 0.1186/s12888-020-02707-9.

Useful Information

ADHD charities and organizations – UK

ADHD Foundation: The Neurodiversity Charity

https://adhdfoundation.org.uk

ADDISS: the National Attention Deficit Disorder Information and Support Service

www.addiss.co.uk

ADHD charities and organizations – US

CHADD – Improving the lives of people affected by ADHD

https://chadd.org

Mental Health Charities and organizations

An A to Z of all the mental health charities and organizations in the UK

www.nhs.uk/mental-health/nhs-voluntary-charity-services/charity-and-voluntary-services/get-help-from-mental-health-helplines

Useful ADHD website and publication

ADDitude – Inside the ADHD brain

www.additudemag.com

Recommended wider reading – ADHD in girls

Solden, S. and Frank, M. (2019) *A Radical Guide for Women with ADHD: Embrace Neurodiversity, Live Boldly and Break through Barriers*. Oakland, CA: New Harbinger Publications.

Steer, J. (ed.) (2021) *Understanding ADHD in Girls and Women*. London: Jessica Kingsley Publishers.

Recommended wider reading – autism in girls

Castellon, S. (2020) *The Spectrum Girl's Survival Guide*. London: Jessica Kingsley Publishers.